I Now Pronounce You Parent

I Now Pronounce You Parent

What Other Books Don't Tell You About Babies

Pat Baker

Baker Book House

Grand Rapids, Michigan 49506

ISBN: 0-8010-0850-6

Printed in the United States of America

To

Nelson and Pamela Bultmann
parents of

Julia

This book
expresses the belief
I have in you
as parents

Thank You

Julia

for changing *my* life
by your being

Linda

for taking
many brief recesses from
from mothering
to edit this book

Precious Moms and **Dads**

for arranging your impossible schedules
to share
your first experiences in parenting

Contents

Dear Mom

If you knew the ages of my children, you might ask how I even have the nerve to write a book about mothers and their babies. I must tell you that I had my babies during an era of no disposable diapers, no natural childbirth classes (*What's a LaMaze?*), and no information on how to breast-feed babies successfully (*How do you pronounce LaLeche?*). The only baby book for easy reference was written by Dr. Spock. The two roles of a father were to contribute to the conception of the baby and to pace around the waiting room until a masked stranger came to tell him that he had become a father.

Even if I had read dozens of baby books, gone to lectures concerning childbirth and child rearing, observed and worked with other babies, and listened to everyone's advice, none of these experiences would have completely prepared me for being a mother. Only being on the job twenty-four hours a day could teach me how it was going to be.

After one of my daughters had been married for a while she asked me, "Mom, how can a couple know when they're ready to have a baby?" That was a difficult question because my answer would not necessarily comply with today's mothers' ideas. I was forced to remember back to my era once more. It was a less complicated decision then. What that particular time period lacked in information, it made up for in simplicity of choice.

At that time becoming a parent was the natural outgrowth of marriage. There were two options for a married woman: She could keep working in her profession (which usually amounted to being a secretary or a school teacher), or she could stop working and have a baby. I didn't know the full implications of my decision to have a baby; I believe many people don't. I do believe that God has a plan for each person's life, and part of His plan for my life included having babies. Human beings have the unique ability to make the choices that are right for them.

This book is my way of coming into your home to give you, as new parents, an injection of support. I want to help you see the basics that are involved in taking care of a baby, the eternal values that go along with parenting, and the way to feel good about being a parent. I want to relate to you as you try to comfort your crying baby, be your company after all your extra help is gone, and sit by you at night when the room is dark and everyone else is asleep. I want you to believe that you can relax and enjoy yourself even when you're worried that your baby's breathing seems erratic, even when you're trying to decide if those cries are because your child is wet, hungry, or just needs to be held in your arms.

I want to thwart your tendency to be critical when you expect too much from yourself and when you begin to think you aren't a good mother. I want you to know that it's all right when your efforts in all your roles don't work out the way you had hoped they would. I want the words in this book to be reassuring and positive, to tell you some of the things to expect from the busy years ahead of you.

Even though my house now contains few items that remind me of my years as a full-time mother, the influence of those young lives still penetrates the walls . . . and I feel so blessed. This is my desire for you as parents.

My years of being a parent included many pleasant experiences, and I believe they should be shared. That's one of my reasons for writing this book. I also have one more reason for sharing the whole, uncensored story of parenting with you. I have been hearing and reading more and more often about married couples deciding not to have babies. That frightens me.

Therefore, I want to get in my high bid for parenting in order to counteract this new trend.

Babies do change lives. We make a total investment of our lives when we decide to bring children into our homes. As I have recalled those busy years as a young mother, thought seriously about the changes that occurred in my life, and realized the total investment I made, I have come to a most staggering conclusion about babies and their worth. *Babies dare us to remain in our selfish state while, at the same time, demanding that we do all the endless things required of us as parents. These requirements, induced by tiny helpless babies, produce the maturing of our selflessness.*

Love,
Pat

1

In Defense of Parenting

Either you are a parent, you're expecting a baby, or you're thinking about having one. How wise you are! Until recently, it was always assumed that married couples would have babies. There was no postscript to that assumption . . . until lately. After hours of researching, observing, and listening, I realize that there are existing options, as well as oppositions, to parenting. They're real, and some of them are legitimate.

I do not believe, however, that this new trend is affecting most couples. And while evidence shows that organized groups are actively engaged in discouraging parenthood, the pro-parenthood advocates have remained silent too long. They must take the initiative and convey their convictions as strongly.

The idea of optional parenthood has some value, but certain statements or ideas seem shallow. Many of these ideas, I feel, come from influential persons who have not experienced and/or enjoyed parenthood, and what has never been personally experienced or enjoyed, many times cannot be shared objectively. Whatever their reasons for feeling so strongly against parenting, I come to its defense. I present the positive side of having babies as opposed to not having them.

You may not feel that this chapter has anything to do with you if you've already decided to become parents, but I believe all of us need to be acutely aware of this growing trend of optional parenthood. You need to be ready to defend, if necessary, the worth of parenting so that future married couples will not make a decision that they may regret later, after the child-bearing years have passed.

What Are the Options?

Have you ever stopped to wonder what social influences are making parenthood an option? All of us are participants in a rapidly changing, progressive world. We are witnessing an era that could be termed the "Self Age" or the "All for Me" generation. It is an "Age of Self-Indulgence," a period when most of us are looking after our own interests, not someone else's. There is a subtle pulling away from anything or anyone that would keep us from having the time to reach our goals and from having sufficient finances to do what WE want to do.

As stated in the preface of this book, "Babies dare us to remain in our selfish state. . . ." This challenge stands in total opposition to the "Self Age" and is difficult for many modern couples to swallow.

Today's married couples are often frustrated; others frightened. They sincerely do not want to add to the problem of overpopulation. (Articles are already appearing, bringing us proof that this is not and will not be a problem.) Couples do not want to be guilty of decreasing the world's food supply or of using up all the natural resources by bringing more children into the world. Other couples are uncertain. They are asking themselves, "Do we want to curb our social life?" Others are career-oriented. They receive much satisfaction from developing and using their intellect and in devoting their time to important social issues. They do not feel that they can develop to their fullest potential if they have to share their energies with children. They feel that if they use up their energy caring for children, they will not be able to contribute fully to society's needs.

Couples ask themselves the following questions: How will having babies affect our marriage? Will babies draw us closer together, or could they pull us apart? Do we want to share each other with another life? Would we share equally the responsibility of caring for a baby?

A researcher claims that most couples are more satisfied in their marriages before their children are born. He states that many marriages reach a low point, when the children are in their school years. When these children are old enough to leave home, another high point in the couple's relationship is experienced.

I would like to add to these observations. Anytime a baby is added to a home, there are hours of hard work involved. This busy time will not keep you from doing many things with and for each other. Strangely enough, this can become a time of steady strengthening in your marriage bond. When you decide to have babies you step into a realm of a different kind of love, another stage of marriage. You will not only be sharing life with each other, but you will enhance your love by sharing it with another life. As far as your relationship with each other is concerned, you will engage in hurried kisses, impromptu I love you's, and stolen intimate moments; you will feel gratitude for uninterrupted silences. These acts and feelings are all necessary and meaningful displays of affection that create the strengths involved in loving one another. But remember: these brief, hurried up interludes do not last forever.

When you become a parent you begin to *learn to modify your life.* Babies don't stop purposes; they don't demolish goals or your usefulness. Babies create new purposes, new goals, new challenges. As you learn to modify your schedule, activities, and personal interests, you'll begin to concentrate on the things that have the most value. You'll leave off those that can be picked up, if the interest is still there, at a later date. You won't be required to go into social retirement. You'll still have your involvements, but they will be carried out in lesser degrees and for shorter lengths of time. Your interests will remain active, but total involvement is "shelved" for a time. You do yourself and your babies a great injustice if you feel that you have to hibernate and stagnate during their growing years. Children will learn by seeing you actively pursuing your own interests.

It is a false idea that after you start having babies you must neglect your personal needs and that your total interest must be consummated within the walls of your home. You will continue to socialize. You will continue to be moderately involved in outside activities, and you will also develop new interests. You'll be doing practically the same things you did before; the only difference will be that you will have another person to consider and include.

Do babies slow you down? Yes, very much . . . at first . . . but all of us recognize and understand that babies do not remain helpless forever. They grow up . . . a phenomenon of nature. From the day they are born they begin the gradual process of evolving from total dependence to later years of total independence. This is most difficult to believe when that new baby takes up so much of your time.

What will you have to give up now that you're a parent? Nothing, completely. Privacy? Not altogether. Leisure time? Not always. Fulfillment? Never. Again, moderation must be emphasized. You will have time for privacy but not always when you want it nor for long periods. You will still experience leisure time but in shorter spans. And parents who don't believe that they can be fulfilled while they are engaged in guiding another life should reevaluate their definition of "fulfillment."

Parenting starts by demanding most of your energies, both physically and mentally. It's a concentrated effort to care for a newborn baby. It may be that you have never before given yourself as completely to any endeavor. But at the corner of your mind you must recognize that you are a vital part of a life that has the potential of "becoming" . . . a life that will not always need you as it does those first several weeks. Knowing this can help make those first weeks full of cherished moments. You have this small, snuggly, helpless human being needing you to be the complete provider of its needs. Babies, who become children and then adults, eventually satisfy their own needs, establish their own relationships, and work toward their own achievements. They will begin to take responsibilities upon themselves similar to yours and regeneration will continue.

The Waiting Period

Perhaps the major question you face is not, should we have babies, but when should we have them? You may want more maturity before you take on the responsibility of another life; that is commendable. You may not think of yourselves as parent material. You are maturing more slowly than others in relation to the idea of home and parenthood.

Because of the economic structure of our world, you may feel strongly about completing your education before you start a family, not wanting to involve babies in your schooling experiences. Coupled with this notion is the desire to have sufficient time to establish a career, especially if you are concerned about returning to your profession after the birth of your baby.

Finances play an important part in the waiting game. Your goal may be to attain substantial material gain before you have a baby. A sure way of obtaining that goal is for both of you to work. You may not want to have outstanding debts before the babies start to arrive because of the uncertainty of the costs involved with adding family members. The higher your goals, the longer you will probably wait to have your babies.

One of the strongest and most refreshing reasons I have heard expressed by married couples who are deciding to wait to have babies is that they want time to get better acquainted with each other. They want to become responsible toward each other before they start to transfer a portion of their love and responsibility to a baby. They consider this a bonding time, a sealing of their commitment to each other. It is a firming up time before member number three arrives. This is a healthy choice for any marriage, a positive reason to delay having babies.

Couples who are waiting to have babies openly tell anyone how they enjoy their freedom while they are responsible only for themselves. They successfully ignore hints from in-laws and well-meaning friends. Without exception, these same couples can in no way conceal their excitement when they find out they are going to be parents. They feel that they are now ready to witness and to be a part of the miracle of birth. This readiness is reason enough to warrant their personal, private decision to wait to become parents.

"Let's Do It!"

At the beginning of your marriage you are totally satisfied with each other. You don't feel that you are missing out on anything by choosing not to have babies right away. Another level of marriage occurs when you decide to make your union even more complete. You talk, and you plan. You weigh the pros and cons, and together you decide to create a new life in your likeness in the way provided by God to achieve immortality. You feel you are ready to guide and influence a new life that would have eternal value. You are now given the opportunity to impart an inheritance of moral and spiritual beliefs. You take the best from both of your parents' teachings and as one mother said, "begin to improve the stock."

There is no conceivable way that you, as newly inducted, expectant parents, can comprehend the years of responsibility that will be yours. You can listen to veteran parents, read current child-care publications, and dream; but you will have variables that will be unique to your family and that no one will have the proper insight to share with you beforehand.

One point I hope to make is that parental responsibilities do take hours of hard work, but anything that has priceless value is always accompanied by hard work. The satisfaction of long working hours comes as babies begin to respond to the good life you are introducing.

All the subtle hints I can give you about parenting could never adequately describe just how ecstatic you'll be when your baby begins to respond to you with fragile smiles and laughter. You wouldn't completely believe me if I told you how you'll appreciate getting eight hours of uninterrupted sleep, eating a hot meal, or having a working washer and dryer until you have to do without one of them. I could tell you that you will learn to accept stretch marks, varicose veins, jelly and/or teethmarks on furniture, and chubby handprints on freshly painted walls; but I have a feeling that you will have to find out for yourself.

In the years ahead of you, you will involuntarily become a teacher, nurse, seamstress, counselor, chauffeur, chef, den mother, homeroom chairperson, and what seems to be a lifetime member of PTA. Only through daily experience and growing self-control will you learn to speak softly instead of scream, smile when it would be simpler to cry, persevere when you feel like giving up the whole idea of motherhood . . . momentarily anyway! You will have days when you feel you've given 100 percent of yourself and you haven't gotten much in return. At the same time, between the lines of faithful daily living, you will realize that you are doing something valuable with your life and for your child. That is all you will ever need to know.

My Decision . . . and Why

I had an extremely happy childhood. There is no doubt in my mind that my parents loved my sister and me. They were fair to us and allowed us to grow up to be our own persons. I do not recall any unpleasant experiences that had a lasting effect on my later years. My father and mother enjoyed being parents. They were responsible for their children, and they were generous with their love. They administered adequate discipline and showed respect for the uniqueness of our lives. They did not try to glorify parenthood; they were naturals at it. They gave their children proper attention, and at the same time they continued to fulfill their own goals in their adult world. They didn't do things for and with their children because they felt they had to or someone told them they should. I want to believe that they did all of these things because they liked the idea of sharing the good things of life with us.

I had many warm times with my family. I have structured my life as a parent around the basic beliefs that my parents shared with me because I know they work.

I'm sure my parents made sacrifices for me, but after I became a parent, I had to ask myself, "Is this action really a sacrifice when it involves my children?" To an outsider it may look as though parents are sacrificing, but it isn't that at all. It's being perfectly content with owning a secondhand car, wearing last year's fashions, having a smaller house, planning less expensive vacations in order to provide DPT shots, corrective shoes, educational toys, clothes for growing bodies, birthday parties, piano and tennis lessons. What seems to be a sacrifice is actually an extension of love to one's own flesh and blood in the purest form.

Even with my parents' effective, indirect teachings about parenthood, I have had difficult times trying to visualize myself as an effective parent. My most prominent clue that I made the right decision about having babies is that I have had no regrets. I have experienced a unique dimension of living since I have shared my life with other lives.

Jesus shared His life with children while He lived on earth. He loved them. He knew that children would be our greatest teachers if we would allow them to be. His plan was for each of us to enter the world not as complicated adults, but as tiny, insignificant beings, full of potential and teachers in our own right.

Jesus used examples of children many times when He wanted to teach adults significant truths. When His disciples began pushing the children aside in a crowd, Jesus insisted that the children be allowed to come to Him. When He performed the miracle of the feeding of the five thousand, He chose to use the lunch of a willing child. He took children into His arms and placed His hands upon their heads and blessed them.

I can envision Him holding children, looking into their eyes, and seeing the value of His creation. On several occasions He said that we must become as little children. He was saying that we must have the faith of little children in order to accept the eternal plan He has for each life.

He viewed children as gifts with spiritual value. "Children are a gift from God, they are his reward" (Ps. 127:3, LB). "Look at all those children! There they sit around the dinner table as vigorous and healthy as young olive trees. That is God's reward to those who reverence and trust him" (Ps. 128:3-4 LB).

The Scriptures view the joys of motherhood through Mary, Jesus' mother; Elizabeth, mother of John; Jocobed, mother of Moses; Hannah, mother of Samuel. These mothers were chosen not only to conceive and give birth, but also to influence their children, to love them and to eventually give them up so that they could have a lasting effect upon the world. What fulfillment they experienced!

In the Book of Genesis we read that after God created man and woman and blessed them, He issued this command, "Be fruitful, and multiply, and replenish the earth . . ." (Gen. 1:28, KJV). With this commandment He implanted within us the desire to reproduce ourselves. I cannot believe that God would command this if He didn't expect it to be carried out. Possibly, we can only see having babies at face value, but procreation was to have far-reaching effects because it was absolutely the only part of God's creation that would have eternal substance. Everything else in creation would be subject to time, but not human life . . . it was to be eternal. This should give all of us an idea of the importance God has placed on procreation.

Something very important is being lost in our earthly progress. Many people cannot seem to comprehend the spiritual value of having babies. These children are meant to be spiritual gifts from God. A minority of persons believe that children get in the way of progress, that they contribute to using up the finite resources, that relationships are more satisfying without them, that adults can affect more lives if they are not family centered, that they do not want to contribute to the world's pollution problems by adding to the present population, that by not having children they will be actively helping to reduce the energy crisis. The natural outgrowth of these beliefs will be a less crowded world. I must add to these man-made statements. God, who created everything, would not have commanded that man replenish the earth if He thought it would bring a significant imbalance in the order of nature.

I have been an active participant in God's plan of procreation.

I have accepted each of our babies as gifts from God. I can honestly share with you that my faith in God has grown because I've had babies. There were times when I discovered that I couldn't do what I had to do as a parent without spiritual guidance. In my inadequacies, my unsureness, and my weaknesses, God became my strength, my common sense, and my wisdom. There were days when I had to make quick decisions and days when weariness overtook me. There were times when I wondered about the immensity of my role. There were evenings when I stepped into the rooms of my sleeping children and all my heart could express was, "Thank you, Lord. Thank you for letting me be a parent to these precious lives." I have felt needed and loved. These are the gifts from my children.

As I view those three young adult lives now, I can see what they're accomplishing in their lives. I have fleeting flashbacks of the busy growing-up years with them, and I can truthfully say that even through all of my mistakes, limitations, frustrations, joys, and pleasures, "It has been good." They have now forgotten many of my mistakes. Most of the time, they had no idea how limited I felt; they didn't recognize my frustrations. All the joys and pleasures we shared together are remembered, however, and that's what made it "good."

The remainder of this book is my way of giving you my support for what you are doing as parents.

2

I Now Pronounce You Husband and Wife and Parent

There is no mathematical equation to prove that when the two of you are joined together in marriage you become one. The extent and reality of oneness doesn't surface until you actually share your lives together.

A sharing relationship like this can't be compared to the time when you used to leave your date at the door. The relationship is defined by living together, by having direct or indirect contact with each other twenty-four hours a day. It's seeing how the other partner looks when you get up mornings. It's patiently sifting out the bad characteristics to discover the good ones. It's relying on each other's strengths and coping with or tactfully improving the weaknesses. It's creating situations you know will make the other one happy. It's hurting together, sharing disappointments with each other, celebrating accomplishments together, discovering one another's secret dreams, and relishing time spent together. It's experiencing the spontaneity of living with the person you love—going to see a movie together, having friends over, taking late night walks in the snow or rain, going out to eat, renting a secluded cabin for a weekend to recreate the tenderness of your love and commitment. In all these ways, and so many more, you are living out the oneness relationship.

You didn't fully realize that the decision you made to share your lives together would lead to more decisions. Although the scheduling differs with every married couple, eventually the time will come when both of you decide you're ready to bring a new life into your union. At first you won't completely understand how this decision will change your relationship. One effect you can be sure of: you will develop a new dimension in your love for each other. You cannot comprehend, however, what it feels like to have a baby born into your home until you experience it personally.

You will probably begin the decision-making process by generalizing about whether you are ready to have a baby and whether this would be the right time. The subject may start to come up more frequently, accompanied by the question, "Should we or shouldn't we?" Maybe you will stop being as careful as you had been before. You may "forget" to take your usual precautions. In the back of both of your minds you want to conceive. The inevitable conception is when the new dimension in love begins.

Green Mornings

When several young mothers were asked if they devised a unique way of announcing their pregnancy to their husbands, one said, "There was no way to keep it a secret. It became obvious when I started leaning over bathroom stools, making quick exits from meetings, carrying crackers in every purse, and growing pale when someone mentioned the word "food." Each of these women was able to laugh (some were only able to smile) about having morning sickness . . . after the ordeal was over.

You may be one of the fortunate young women who does not have morning sickness with her pregnancy. But for every one like you, there are ten mothers who have varying degrees of it. Morning sickness is an indescribable feeling that starts at the base of the stomach and travels up into the mouth. Some women feel too sick to vomit; others feel too sick not to. If you are one of these favored women, you may want to linger in bed without moving for as long as you can because you know what's going to happen when you put your feet on the floor. There's something about putting your body in a vertical position that starts the process.

Your husband may stand by helplessly and try to offer comfort. "I'm sorry. Would you like for me to fix you a piece of. . . ." Before he can say "toast" you may already be in the bathroom wailing, "Don't mention food and don't touch me!!" Your husband may begin to rationalize. He thinks that if you have a change of scenery, get away from your daily routine, you'll "forget."

One young husband planned what he thought would be a fun weekend in another city. His wife told him that she didn't think it would be wise to go. They went anyway. Her later comment was, "I threw up all over Kansas City." Another husband chartered a private plane, and even with his wife telling him what was going to happen, they went flying. He was not prepared for how the trip in the plane affected his newly pregnant wife. Obviously, getting away doesn't lessen morning sickness, telling unsuspecting friends and co-workers that you have the flu doesn't help, and thinking "I'm going to die" offers no immediate relief.

One of the biggest aggravators of this condition is food. There are mothers today who still have to avoid the sight or smell of particular foods. For several years after our second child was born, my husband kept asking me to buy pork steaks, but I kept forgetting. I told myself that pork wasn't good for us to eat. Then I figured out the psychological reason that made me forget to buy the steaks. When I was pregnant, we had pork steaks often. As soon as I would put the meat in the skillet, I would become nauseated. I would run to the farthest room in the house from the kitchen and stay there until I thought it was time to brown the other side of the meat. Even when I served it,

I could hardly eat it. I have begun to serve pork steaks again, but the memory still lingers.

One young mother shared that even the smell of the kitchen made her sick. She got up each morning and as she was getting ready to go to work, her husband went into the kitchen and prepared her a thermos of hot tea and a generous day's supply of crackers. In the evenings she would sit in the living room and give her husband cooking instructions for their meal. She felt guilty that he was doing "her" work, but his compassionate reply was, "Anyone who looks as miserable as you do *needs* help!"

Can you imagine how the smell of egg salad might affect an already sick, pregnant woman? One survived to tell about her experience. "One morning when I was sitting in my cubicle at work I began to smell egg salad. I thought I could handle it, but the strong smell persisted. I unashamedly got up and sniffed in each person's cubicle until I found the man who had brought the egg salad sandwich for his lunch. I couldn't ask him to throw it away, so I did the next best thing. I asked him to put it in his car. When he saw my weakened condition, he took it to his car immediately."

Although it doesn't stop morning sickness from occurring, it's good for expectant mothers to know why it happens. During the first three months of pregnancy, the placenta is being formed. The hormone progesterone, which is present in the mother's body, takes charge in order to favor the nesting of the fertilized egg. This creates a hormonal imbalance in the mother's system; the imbalance causes morning sickness. This knowledge may not relieve your condition, but at least you know that what you're going through is not fatal. Many doctors suggest that too many liquids during this time may increase the nausea. Placing crackers by the bed at night and eating some before getting up each morning might relieve you to some extent.

When you've gotten past thinking that you have a virus, when you've ruled out food poisoning, a tumor, or nerves, you'll want to verify your suspicions with a doctor. Personalities are an important consideration as you look for a doctor. You may like the all-professional approach, or you may relate better to a doctor who is easy to talk with, compassionate, and willing to take time to answer your questions. Some doctors deliver so many babies they become desensitized to first-time-around mothers. You may feel you have some knowledge of what is happening to your body, but many things will still be blurry and need to be defined.

Some doctors feel it is important to take time with you to let you know about various kinds of deliveries and anesthetics that can be used, routines they follow in delivery, etc. Many times, even the busiest doctors will talk with you after each examination to see if you have further questions. Write down the questions you want to ask your doctor so you won't forget. Having questions answered will help you know what to expect from your pregnancy. You can go home, relax, and enjoy your pregnancy without worry. You'll soon begin to realize the miracle that is growing inside of you. As you watch the baby's progress, you'll want to do all that you can to give your baby the best possible introduction into the waiting world.

Do It Your Way

You're going to have a baby. You and your husband probably laughed and/or cried together when you found out that you were definitely pregnant. Perhaps it didn't quite soak in at first (sometimes it takes the full nine months to get used to the idea), but something totally new is happening to you. You've seen and known other pregnant women, your friends have talked about it, but now it's different. It's more special than you ever realized it could be. Something deep inside you instinctively begins to send out messages that you and your husband are in the process of creating a responsibility . . . one that will require total commitment and massive doses of your time and energy.

There are so many new things for you to learn, so many decisions to make. Two decisions that must be made from the beginning because of the the prior preparation involved are what type of delivery you will want and whether or not you will breast-feed your baby.

After choosing her doctor, one young mother found out that he delivered most of the babies by unmedicated childbirth. She was afraid that he would try to talk her into having her baby in this manner. She talked with him and said, "I have this one little problem; I can't stand pain!!" When he knew about her fear he reassured her that he would use an anesthetic during the delivery and make her as comfortable as possible.

Along with many young mothers, however, you may choose to have your baby while you are awake, alert, and able to assist in the natural process of childbirth. You and your husband may attend classes and receive instructions on what to expect during labor and delivery. Even if you choose to have your baby by another method, it would benefit both you and your husband to attend these classes. A hospital tour to introduce you to the surroundings of the labor, delivery, and recovery rooms is usually a part of the class. The class will also include lectures on the anatomy of the uterus, cervix, fetus, mucous plug, placenta, etc. The class will emphasize to you that this birth will be a team effort of the husband-coach and the mother-to-be. The coach has a prestigious job; he is equally important during labor and delivery. Although these classes will take time from you and your husband's busy schedules, the results are invaluable. Fears are diminished, a common knowledge of what is to come is gained, and a sense of being in this together is shared. Many doctors suggest that you start attending these classes during the seventh month of the pregnancy so that you will recall more clearly what you have learned when the delivery occurs.

One nurse said that there is no comparison between the reactions of women who have taken these classes and those who haven't. A mother shared that before she conceived she had never been around women with babies nor had much knowledge of how babies were born. Her motives for attending childbirth classes were to help her know what to expect when her baby was born. "If I hadn't gone to those classes I would've been terrified," she related. "The class also encouraged my husband to share this time in our lives together."

The other decision that should be made in advance is whether or not you will breast-feed your baby. Whether you ask them or not, well-meaning parents, relatives, friends, and total strangers will probably share with you their personal knowledge of either breast-feeding or bottle-feeding. It's too bad that expectant mothers are often influenced by latest feeding trends. You are the baby's mother. You have the prerogative to do what pleases you.

If you choose to breast-feed your baby you'll need to begin prenatal breast care. Flat nipples should be massaged with a cream that contains lanolin in order to make them stand out. To toughen the nipples, some doctors suggest washing them daily with a coarse washcloth. Also, when the time and place seem proper to you, go braless. This will allow your nipples to touch your clothing, causing them to toughen up.

The positive points in breast-feeding are: you always have two built-in mechanisms with you; your milk is always the right temperature; the milk feeds antibodies, which confer immunity, into your baby's body; your breasts always comply with the law of supply and demand. The milk is premixed, raw, fresh, sterile, easy to digest. It reduces gas disorders and is economical. Nursing mothers all agree that you can't improve on nature. The cost involved in breast-feeding is your time. The only people involved in the feeding process are you and your baby. One doctor told a young mother, "If you have anything better to do, don't breast-feed your baby." Many mothers decide they have nothing better to do!

If you would like to have more information about breast-feeding, ask your doctor for some booklets on the subject or write LaLeche League International, Inc., 9616 Minneapolis Avenue, Franklin Park, Illinois 60131. This group has published a book entitled: *The Womanly Art of Breast-feeding.* It can be purchased or checked out from a public library.

Some minimal expense is involved in bottle-feeding. Most any baby book will tell you what equipment you will need.

Bottle-feeding requires a preparation, warm-up, and clean-up time, but if you choose to go this route, you will automatically work these steps into your schedule. Two positive aspects of bottle-feeding are that you can be relieved of some of the feedings and you'll know exactly how much milk your baby is getting.

Whatever your decision, breast-feeding or bottle-feeding, you can produce a happy baby who is both emotionally and physically healthy. It's up to you to decide which procedure will be most comfortable for you.

You have approximately nine months to prepare for your child's birth. You had no real reason to learn anything about pregnancy until you became pregnant yourself, but now you discover that such a special happening is worth much thought and preparation. Educate yourself about what's happening inside your body. Keep asking your doctor questions. "Why should I keep my weight down?" "What will happen if I don't?" "I eat fruit, so why am I still constipated? What can I do about it?" "Why do I feel tired all the time?" "Is it normal to have high and low moods?"

Saturate yourself, not only with what your doctor tells you and what other mothers share with you, but also by reading books about the prenatal period. There are many excellent books on the market and in public libraries on the subject. Talk with positive parents; avoid those parents who have the habit of being totally negative, who have not accepted the challenge, privilege, and commitment of parenting. Enjoy every moment of anticipation during these months.

"I Think It's Time!"

You're eight months, three and three-fourths weeks pregnant. How are you feeling? "FAT!" You've cleaned your house; you have the washing folded and the ironing put away. You're sick of your maternity clothes. It's been awhile since you could tie your shoes so you give in, even at this late date, and buy a pair that don't require tying. You've had your suitcase packed for so long everything in it is wrinkled. Your husband can't do or say anything right. He keeps saying you look great, but when you walk by a full-length mirror you immediately dismiss his statements. You're so bored you've started making Q-tips out of toothpicks and cotton. "Why isn't this baby doing something?" "Is something wrong?" You check back nine months on the calendar. "Did we count wrong?" "Have I gone past my due date?" You're disgusted with every mother in the world whose baby came on time or two weeks early.

You debate whether to call your doctor once more, even though you have an appointment to see him the next day. Before you start to dial you wonder if his patience with you is growing thin, so you hang up the receiver. In the midst of all your anxiety, you notice that you have started spotting. *"Is this normal?"* There's a twinge in your lower back. *"The baby must be shifting."* You have a slight pain. *"Maybe this is it!"* Strange reactions begin to occur with the first suspicion of labor. Women start making beds, filling green stamp books, polishing their nails, cleaning closets, washing dirty dishes, mopping floors, and wondering all the time if they're experiencing only gas pains. Husbands start shaving and showering. Some shout; others are obviously silent and/or pale. Finally, you are sure the moment has come to make the famous statement, "I think it's time. . . ."

The night before our first child was born I awoke from a deep sleep. As I was trying to turn over in bed without my husband's help, I experienced a pain in my lower back that I had not felt before. I automatically got up and went into the bathroom as I had done so often in the last few weeks. Then I felt another pain. *"Maybe I didn't feel it? Am I awake?"* Still another pain. I remembered reading that if the pains were regular, I'd better put Plan A into action. I timed my pains. I was having them every five minutes. After about a half hour had elapsed, I knew that what I'd been waiting nine months for was going to culminate that night. I was going to have a baby! I went in to wake the unsuspecting expectant father. We knew so little, but our lack of knowledge didn't keep us from anticipating the joys of our imminent childbirth.

After a nine-month run at pregnancy you probably feel reasonably prepared for any discomfort that might occur during the next uncertain hours. You check with your husband to see how he's holding up. *"He's doing fine."* He picks up the suitcase that contains the wrinkled clothes, and the two of you begin a journey that you'll share together for the rest of your lives, a journey that will involve another significant human being. The drama of the next few hours has as many different beginnings and endings as there have been births.

When I announced that it was time to go to the hospital to have our third baby, my husband jumped up, threw the book he was reading across the floor, and rushed me to the car. Since we lived thirty minutes from the hospital, he was anxious to get me there. Halfway through the trip my water broke, and I vaguely remember the color instantly draining from my husband's face. I think he was mumbling, "I knew I should have paid more attention to that section titled, 'If You Can't Get to the Hospital in Time.'" He was sending out silent messages, daring me to have the baby in the car. As soon as we got to the hospital, he left me in the car, ran into the emergency entrance, and told a nurse, "There's a woman out in the car having a baby!" I have often wondered whether she realized he was my husband.

I am so pleased with the progress that has been made through the years allowing husbands to share all the stages of labor and delivery with their wives. My memories are always of total isolation from anything or anyone familiar to me. I experienced an intimate process, and I didn't have my husband to share it with me. I was in the labor room alone while he was filling out hospital forms, trying to read *Pilgrim's Progress,* pacing in the waiting room, and wondering what was happening to me. But today your husband can choose to get in on the action. Most husbands are extremely helpful during this time, although they may react differently during the action scenes. One husband kept handing his wife the newspaper "to help you forget what's happening." Another husband kept falling asleep. His wife couldn't believe this reaction when he *knew* she was having their baby.

One of the end results of participation in natural childbirth classes is the total concentration you learn. You and your husband are very much aware of each stage of the birth process. There is pain involved, but you cooperate with each contraction. Your minds are not on yourselves as you focus totally on getting your baby born. Finally, there's that one final push. After nine months of waiting both of you get your first glimpse of a new, flawless human being. Although you may actually see a flat face, misshapen head, upside-down looking ears, wrinkled and red skin, you'll believe you've been handed a perfect ten.

The intensity of first remarks varies. "I went through all of that for this?" "He's so ugly." "This child is mine." "When they put the baby on my chest I felt relief and began to weep. I touched her for a while." "We both giggled. She was so beautiful." "WE did it!" "He looks like Winston Churchill."

You may admit that you don't automatically love your baby. You are strangers. Your baby has yet to become a natural extension of you, the new parents. It may be a matter of hours before love will evolve in a way you never knew would be possible. You begin to look at and touch your baby, and you know that this little, new body has consummated your union as husband and wife. Maybe love will begin a little later when you acknowledge that there is a Supreme Purpose for this birth. The Heavenly Father, in His generous, all-knowing way, knew the depth of love this birth would add to your lives as you begin to give large chunks of yourselves away to another human being.

3

What Do You Do With a Baby?

When you get home you'll probably keep saying your baby's name over and over because it still doesn't quite fit. But the more you say it, the more it attaches itself to this new personality. You and your husband are now in charge. You have the privilege of reducing your world to your new family during the next weeks. You have no one to think of except you, your husband, and your baby. No one is more important at this time. You are not responsible for the relative or friend who has come to help. Neither are you responsible for entertaining those who will be coming to see the baby. You and your baby are your *only* responsibility. If you play the perfect hostess as you've always done, you may find you are over-extending your energies. Let someone else do the entertaining for a while.

It's during this time that your baby will decide to cry at night and sleep during the day or vice versa. During this transition period it may comfort you to know that new parents all over the world are wondering what they're supposed to do with their babies. What benefits could possibly come from someone whose head is wobbly and whose eyes won't focus, but who is quite prolific at crying and wetting. This little power bundle, weighing in under ten pounds, will exhaust the strongest, challenge the most intellectual, and frustrate the most patient. Your baby has come into the world with a fresh supply of raw materials and you, the parents, will refine them and make them valuable. All you see right now is that limber, fragile body, but inside that body is the potential to become a unique individual; your baby expects your help to accomplish this task.

Mothers, how are you feeling? Happy? Apprehensive? Relaxed? Tired? Already experienced some unsure moments? Remember when you were first married, or when you were interviewed for your first job? After you settled into your marriage and your job, you became more comfortable with them. A new baby produces a similar situation. You have a new job, and the more you learn what is expected of you and what to expect from your baby, the more efficient you'll become. You will not be fair to yourself if you think you have to know everything about parenting within the first twenty-four hours. Nature has endowed you with certain parental instincts, and each day you work with your baby you'll perfect those instincts.

Try to avoid opinions of other people. Defy comparing your baby with other babies the same age as yours. You have your own instincts working for you. It is also a good idea to have one or two reliable resource people whom you feel free to call on. This may be an interested neighbor, a close friend, or possibly a visiting nurse.

Your baby will take most of your time, but there's something you must know and keep reminding yourself. The first few weeks babies are totally, completely, absolutely dependent on their parents. This next part is the crucial part to understand! Even before six months have passed, your baby will show the minute beginnings of independence. So be selfish and enjoy those first few weeks and months when your little one is totally dependent on you.

During this period, particular things will give you concern. Much of this concern will grow from not knowing what to expect from your baby or from yourself. If you are breastfeeding, you may wonder if your milk is satisfying your baby's needs. Try to remember that you'll generally have as much milk as the baby demands. If you worry your baby is nursing too often, remember that frequent nursing stimulates your milk production. There may be days when more milk will be needed. If this happens, you will be able to provide it. The more liquids you drink the better it is for your milk supply. It is usually sufficient for your baby to nurse ten minutes on each breast, but, remember, there are exceptions. It takes some babies longer than others to decide where the milk supply is coming from, and they'll need to be guided. Some babies must feel the nipple on their palate, others need you to gently touch their lips. This will set the natural sucking reflex into action.

Look forward to the nursing times. It's your chance to get some deserved relaxation. Lie on the bed, sit in your most comfortable chair, prop up your feet, turn on some soft music . . . in other words, "baby" yourself while you are nursing your baby. You're worth it! To your baby you are the most important person in the world. What could be more fulfilling to you and more satisfying to your baby? You hold that little body close giving a warm meal and knowing you're providing it. Total relaxation contributes to a good milk supply, a contented baby, and a proud mom. You're actually accomplishing two things in one setting. You are meeting your baby's immediate physical needs, and the sucking releases the hormone, oxitocin, which contracts your uterus. The more your baby sucks, the more contractions you'll have, and the sooner you'll be back to that size 8-10-12-14. . . .

Concerns of New Parents

There's not a more beautiful picture of serenity than a mother holding a baby that is filled, dry, and asleep. But what if the scene shifts? The baby is filled, dry, and NOT asleep but crying. What makes a baby cry? Why does a mother get upset when her baby cries? Marvin Girsh writes in his book, *How to Raise Children in Your Spare Time,* that during the first few months a baby may cry approximately two hours a day. Your baby may decide to get it all over with in two straight hours or may cry intermittently throughout the day. When crying occurs, consider these guidelines. *Confront yourself.* "Why is this upsetting me?" *Assure yourself.* Eighty percent of all the babies ever born do the same thing, and they survived without permanent injury. Crying is not fatal. *Control yourself.* "Okay, you're crying. I'm going to stay with you. (I may cry with you.) It'll be over soon and then all of us can get some rest."

I must confess that I am allergic to 5:00 PM. This allergy developed shortly after our first daughter was born and continued with each baby until the last one was born seven years later. Every evening as the sun started to go down each baby got her clue from somewhere, and she knew it was time to start crying. I never did know why it was always around 5:00. Maybe it was because I was starting the evening meal, or my energy level was low. Perhaps I became more tense as the hour approached and that tension was transferred to my babies.

There are only so many ways to comfort a crying baby. I think I tried every one of them at least a dozen times. I want to share three things that worked for me. Each one helped to comfort my babies . . . and me. First, I put my baby on my shoulder and walked with her. I read several years later that walking created a rocking sensation like she grew accustomed to before she was born. This seemed to soothe her to some extent. At other times, I would place a tiny hot water bottle filled with moderately warm water on the baby's stomach, lay her across my lap, and pat her gently on her back. I thought this might alleviate uncomfortable gas that may have formed while she was nursing. I also got lots of mileage out of my rocking chair. No home with babies should be without one.

As you try some of these methods or others suggested to you, concentrate on your baby. Dismiss from your mind how tired you are and forget other things you need to get done. Salvage what energy you have left to make your baby comfortable. Strangely enough, mothers are always able to gather up sufficient energy when a special need arises. Relief and rest will eventually come to both of you.

Many parents become concerned when their baby sneezes. "Oh, no, a cold already." This, however, is the normal way for a baby's nose to clear itself. Hiccups are extremely aggravating not only to your baby, but also to you. After feeding, burping, and rocking to sleep, you gently place your baby in the crib. The next thing you hear is a hiccup and a cry. Granulated sugar on the back of the baby's tongue or a drink of warm water may bring relief. Most of the time, however, hiccups have to run their course. Hiccups are a normal reaction to being too full or swallowing some air while nursing.

Diaper rash is another concern. My first instructor, my baby's grandmother, had me boil all the soiled diapers in a large pail each day. The next step was to rinse the diapers three times, in fresh water each time. Then I squeezed each diaper by hand and hung them up to dry. Result: Lifetime Diaper Rash Immunity. Since more mothers are using disposable diapers, they should be aware that certain brands contain perfume, which can cause diaper rash. If diaper rash occurs for any reason, one treatment is to mix one teaspoon of boric acid into a cup of water. Wash the baby's bottom with the solution after each diaper change and pat dry. Change diapers frequently since urine contains a high level of ammonia and this acid promotes diaper rash. There are other possible reasons for diaper rash. Your doctor may have already informed you what should be done if it does happen. If the rash becomes severe, don't hesitate to notify your doctor.

"Where Did My Schedule Go?"

You're probably aware of other changes, besides diaper changes, no one bothered to tell you about before you became a parent. Most baby books let you in on certain things to expect from your baby, but they don't let you know how these changes will affect your daily routines.

Mothers accustomed to a strict daily schedule find it more difficult, although not impossible, to adjust their daily routines around the baby. Maybe you have always washed, shopped, and housecleaned on certain days. You've had your meals ready to serve at certain hours, and you've gone to bed and gotten up at a particular time each evening and morning. It was always a workable schedule . . . until your baby came. For some reason you never dreamed just how much everything would change, at least during the first several weeks.

You've already discovered that your baby's days are completely uncomplicated. No such thing as a schedule at first. Someone failed to tell this little person that you would want to get specific things accomplished and therefore lived on a schedule. The baby's view from the crib is just the opposite. Babies are born knowing the bare essentials for survival. Your lives as a new mother and dad are complicated by outside influences and pressures. Your baby's task is not to make things more complicated for you, but to uncomplicate your lives so you can enjoy taking care of this little person's needs.

All of us are creatures of habit. We enjoy doing things our way, trying to fit everything, including people, into our schedules. Of course, your little one isn't aware of this. Your baby does not try to change your schedule out of spite, but out of need. You've been elected to satisfy those needs. It's that simple. Since all of us are basically selfish, we battle this idea that there are times when our babies will invade our privacy. No matter what kind of schedule has been set up, babies know when to start crying. In doing so, they can disrupt even the most general of schedules. They'll start crying when: 1) you're preparing a meal, 2) you're trying to eat the meal you've prepared, 3) you're cleaning up after the meal. They'll wake up when you're ready to go to sleep. They'll sleep when you want them to wake up so you can get to a certain place at a particular time. They'll dirty so many diapers that they'll completely destroy your once-a-week washing schedule.

These are only a few of the instances about which books, doctors, and television programs fail to tell you. I'm sure they assume you'll discover these things for yourself. It has always amused me to watch a television program with a baby as one of the characters. Anytime the baby's parents have a serious discussion, entertain guests, want to read or watch television, or have a candlelight dinner for two, they simply put the baby in its crib; and the baby is never heard from again. What a joke! In reality, the baby often crashes whatever is taking place.

An art worthy of perfecting during these first weeks is the art of enjoying your baby even when your life and schedules are interrupted. Learn to enjoy yourself when eating with your child on your lap or when your deepest sleep between two or three o'clock every morning is interrupted. You may think you don't have the time, but stop whatever you're doing and look, really look, at your baby. Reestablish in your mind the joys already experienced. Be conscious of the fast stages of a baby's growth. Try to imagine how your life was "before-baby." These are days when your baby seems to change by the hour, so consciously enjoy each day's progress. Watch the new things your child does, and remember that you're helping a new life develop.

You won't have to ditch every day's schedule; you may need only to modify it. When you feel total frustration and your accomplishments register zero, perhaps you're expecting too much out of yourself and/or your baby. You'll be inclined to think that you're not getting anything done on any typical day. Are you sure? By what standard are you assuming this? On any given day you will have taken care of all of your baby's needs, put the washer through its paces, straightened the house (or at least parts of it) prepared one warm and simple meal, and sneaked in some time with your husband. None of these things merit public recognition, but every one is extremely important for you and your family.

If it is impossible for you to navigate without the semblance of a schedule, grab one of your few quiet times and make your own personal work lists under the following topics: 1) Things that *have* to be done, 2) Things I would *like* to get done, 3) Things that can wait, and 4) Things to do after child starts to school.

The items listed under topic number one are the things you will always concentrate on getting done. They are the ones that will require most of your attention. Think through the basics, the things that *have* to be done: 1) you have to care for your baby's needs, 2) your family has to eat, 3) certain clothing items have to be washed, and 4) you must have time to relax at different intervals throughout the day. You may be tempted to leave this last item off your list. Don't! Write it down so you won't forget. Every mother has fifteen minutes a day when she can take a walk (do it with the baby), read, or nap (while the baby naps).

Category two might look like this: 1) straighten house, 2) get hair combed and self dressed by noon, 3) give self a manicure, 4) take a shower. Under topic three you might have: 1) sew buttons back on husband's shirts; 2) mate all of husband's navy blue and black socks; 3) change bed linens; 4) clean closet, stove, refrigerator, or do any other type of heavy housework. Under category four you are simply telling yourself to "forget it . . . for a while."

Many mothers are learning to economize with their clothing, gas, and grocery expenditures so someone can come into their homes regularly to catch them up on household chores. This isn't a luxury. It's something good you do for yourself. If your goal is to have time to be a more effective mother, you must include some time for yourself. Mention this when you approach your husband about the possibility of household help. Your budget, however, may be stretched too tightly to even consider it. There is another option, and it's free. Let your husband know that there are some things you haven't been able to get done, and they've started to get to you. Ask him to take charge of the baby for a while so you will be free to get these things done without being interrupted. Keep realistic goals, and don't try to do everything at one time. It usually takes a short while to finish up the things that have been bothering you the most.

"A Mother Is a Persin Too."

A group of second grade children were assigned to write their definition of a mother. One sensitive child wrote, "A mother is a persin too." Why do you unconsciously begin to lose your own identity when your baby is born? Does your identity get lost in piles of diapers that always need washing and folding? Does your loss of self occur when you're trying to plan and prepare meals or disguise scorched ones? Or is it while you're running up and down the aisles in the grocery store, throwing items into your shopping basket so you can hurry back home? Does it get misplaced when you're staying up late with your baby, singing lullabies, rocking the fretful child to sleep?

You do not stop being your unique self when you add another role to your life. Although it is important to be available to your baby's needs, you must also be equally aware of your own needs. Things happened so quickly after the birth of your baby. You were kept busy in the hospital learning how to feed your baby, getting sitz baths and heat lamp treatments for healing stitches, walking to the nursery to make sure your baby wasn't crying, and talking with your visitors. Soon however the hospital stay was over, and you went home.

I had always seen pictures of mothers arriving home from the hospital holding their babies and smiling. I visualized myself doing the same thing when I brought my first daughter home. I was happy, but I was also extremely uncomfortable and weak. I figured the discomfort was from the episiotomy. It wasn't until I had my six-week checkup that my doctor just happened to tell me that he had done some repair work on me during the delivery. I thought, since this was my first baby, that it was normal to have to sit on one hip during the first few weeks after the delivery.

Most mothers are physically uncomfortable and tire easily at first. Besides some of the physical discomforts, they can expect interrupted sleep each night because of the baby's night feedings and irregular sleeping habits. That's why it is so important for you to drop everything during the day when your baby sleeps so you can sleep also. You may rationalize, "Now that I've got the baby to sleep, I'll hurry and get a few things done, and then I'll rest awhile." Don't count on that happening. Your baby may wake up before you have the chance to rest, so reverse your schedule and rest first. Then if your baby decides to take one of those delightful three-hour naps, you can get some work done. Take pride in doing yourself a favor, in doing what is the most important thing.

Fatigue is an unexpected, emotional jolt to many new mothers. Until your baby was born you usually rested when you were tired. You slept in on weekends. If you got sleepy on a lazy afternoon you curled up in a warm place and slept. You took it for granted that you could sleep anytime you wanted or needed to. Why shouldn't you have taken sleep for granted? You had never known it to be any other way . . . until now.

There are people who can function well on small amounts of sleep, but there are others whose mental well-being is highly affected by a lack of sleep. I fell into the second category. One morning after a hectic, sleepless night taking care of a baby who wasn't quite asleep but wasn't awake enough to nurse, I told my husband, "I haven't been happy a day since this baby was born." That was an exaggeration because there had been many good days, but I was tired, and that's how I felt.

Fatigue is detrimental to a new mother's mental health. That's why, if you're one of those women who sleeps lightly and wakes at the least noise, especially all those kinds of noises babies make in their sleep, do not hesitate at anytime to ask for extra help. Let me encourage you. It won't be long until you will be back to "normal" and functioning as you did before your baby was born. Before that happens, however, some of your days will probably look gray, especially after you've gone through a steady succession of sleepless nights.

If you are even halfway a fan of Erma Bombeck I recommend that you buy, borrow, or check out from the public library her book entitled, *I Lost Everything in the Postnatal Depression.* She takes a heavy subject and turns it into a chain of humorous incidents. It can make mothers if not laugh, at least smile at their present situation.

Another thing that may plague you as a new mother is meeting head on for the first time the fact that being a mother is not so glamorous as you thought it would be. You can't forget how happy you were the day you found out you were pregnant, how you and your husband celebrated. Then you began to tell your good news to the world. You could hardly wait to wear your first maternity outfit so the ones you forgot to tell about your pregnancy would know your condition. The excitement continued to build as relatives and close friends gave you baby showers. Even after putting the gifts in their proper places you kept getting them out to look at them. You kept busy buying additional items you felt you would need. You could only dream about what it would be like to care for your baby because you had nothing concrete with which to compare your dreams.

Then you had your baby. You came home, and even though the baby books prepared you in a general way, you never imagined how all the first time things would begin to happen. There is certainly no glamour in dirty diapers, diarrhea, and baby's drool on all of your clothing. You find yourself confined to your home. This isn't because you have to be confined, but you can't seem to muster up the energy it takes to go somewhere. Fatigue and unexpected confinement result in a mother experiencing moderate and, in some cases, severe depression. Never apologize for the way you are feeling. If all you need is rest, make immediate arrangements with the most available person to take care of some of your responsibilities for a while. If you need a brief recess from your parental duties tell your husband or some other willing person that you need some time off. Maybe you've always been able to handle any circumstance without someone else's help, but you find this isn't possible now. Admit that you can't do it alone. In some instances mothers need to seek medical advice. Do not hesitate to seek this kind of help if it becomes necessary.

This sounds like a drab picture, but these things happen in many homes after babies arrive. Mothers are trying to care for their babies as well as get back to functioning as they did before their babies were born. This is the side of parenting that is not revealed in many books, but it must be understood. It can be a frightening time for mothers who are uninformed as to how depression due to fatigue can affect their mental stability.

You and your husband have already had many days of enjoyment with your baby, and there will be more of those days. In order to have them you must be continually sensitive to your needs. Allow yourself the luxury of saying aloud at least once a day that you are special. You are important. You are not only important to your baby and to your husband, but you are also important to yourself. This will give you some incentive to continue to develop your life not only as a mother and wife but as a "persin" too.

Settling In

After a short period of time you will know that you have survived the arrival of this new little stranger in your life. These first few weeks are a settling in time for each of you. You're getting acquainted with a little person who is fast becoming inseparable from your life. You find it difficult to separate your roles as wife, mother, and "persin." Your roles mesh as soon as your baby cries in the early morning hours and continues all the hours in between. You can rise up with all mothers and declare that parenting is all-inclusive in your daily life. It's a simple fact. You can no longer think only of yourself; there is someone else to consider, and that someone will be a part of your life for several years.

Your baby doesn't keep you from doing other things with your life. He asks only to be considered in your plans. Because of your baby, you'll begin to develop, if you haven't already, new friendships with other young parents. You'll share your good and bad days with them. You'll visit in each other's homes and see similar developments. You'll establish lasting bonds with these mother-friends. Your feelings of inadequacy will dissolve as you begin to understand the enormous responsibilities and privileges that are yours and to know that you are capable of handling all of them.

Your baby will bring about many changes in your life, and that's good because it will make you realize that God knows you are capable of handling those changes. Because of this belief in you, He has allowed you to care for another life.

4

And Daddy Makes Three

Your husband's role as father actually begins before the baby is born. After all, he has probably never before witnessed a pregnant woman with morning sickness until you demonstrated it for him. He probably will have difficulty trying to decide if he should stay close by or if he should keep a safe distance until the episode is over for one more morning. There is no way to register the mental anguish he experiences as he tries to decide how to convince you that you are still attractive even after your waistline disappears and you grow new frontage. He's the one you dream, anticipate, and plan with for nine long months. Suddenly all those special moments dissolve into reality when it is time for the two of you to team up and go to the hospital to deliver a newly created human being . . . the extension of your lives.

How New Fathers React

Expectant fathers do as many strange things as expectant mothers when it's time to go to the hospital. When some husbands realize that their wives aren't having gas pains, irrational behavior occurs. You know he isn't rational when you get into the car as calmly and gracefully as possible, and instead of heading toward the hospital, your husband parks the car at a restaurant and stands in line to buy a box of fried chicken or a dozen chocolate doughnuts. Since this is the first trip of this kind for him as well as for you, he probably doesn't realize how much pain you are having or how high your anxiety level has reached. Generally, most couples do arrive at the hospital in time. Any questions you may have about your husband's concern for you and your baby ends when he demonstrates that he remembers practically everything he learned in childbirth classes.

You can only imagine what your husband feels during the birth process as he sees you in pain. He wonders if everything is going as it should, tries to make himself believe that the doctors know what they are doing and questions whether anyone else in the room realizes what a special historical event this is. Finally, the questioning and waiting are over. The birth process is complete.

Until your baby's arrival you did not fully realize how much your husband's presence, encouragement, and tenderness could mean to you. His coaching guided you. You know you couldn't have gotten through it as well without him. Later, you tell him what his being there with you meant.

Every husband's reaction to the phenomenon of birth is different. Your husband may be quiet, laugh, or cry. He will hold his baby and realize, although maybe not fully, that this new form is part of him and you. Your husband has experienced the miracle of birth with you. He was involved, and you are glad!

Changes Husbands Notice

It doesn't take long for new parents to recognize immediate changes in the atmosphere after they arrive home with the baby. From the start there will be many bewildering surprises.

As you combine your physical recuperation with caring for the baby, your husband may openly acknowledge how much work you did around the house before the baby came, especially when he finds himself taking over some of your responsibilities so you can rest. Many new fathers quickly discover that they must fake alertness and productivity at work each day after they've lost hours of sleep the night before. They realize that the spontaneity of living is suddenly over. "You'll never believe all the plans we have to make just to go to buy groceries." There's more of everything around . . . more dirty dishes, more dirty clothes, more unmade beds, and more late meals. Some days, tension is high because of sleepless nights both of you are experiencing. Lack of sleep creates fatigue and fatigue produces the tension. These new tensions can affect the intimacy you shared before the baby came; to what degree depends on the openness you have with each other.

"How's Your Love Life?"

During the first few weeks of your baby's life you may have to struggle to answer this question. How is your love life? You had no way of knowing what kind of changes would take place once the baby was home, and to what extent these changes would affect your love life. You will be especially vulnerable while you are faced with a new role as mother. The seemingly unsurmountable responsibilities could keep you in a state of fatigue for several months. Fatigue can significantly affect your sexual interests and desires at this time.

Before babies are born, couples always have ample time for romantic encounters with each other. The atmosphere for these encounters varies: soft music in a dimly lit room, a secluded place in the country for the weekend, candlelight dinners, special motels, enticing night gowns, freshly cut flowers delivered at the door, and time to fantasize through the day about that special evening with each other . . . all meaningful times in a growing marriage relationship. But for several weeks after the birth of a baby, romantic inclinations come close to extinction.

Then you have your six-week checkup and the doctor tells you that it's all right for you and your husband to resume having intercourse. I've often wondered if doctors know how impossible that statement sounds to a woman who is still trying to work out the formula for being a mother. She might rather hear him say, "I believe you and your husband should wait a little longer." She is in a state of constant fatigue, and she doesn't feel that she has the strength to perform one more act, even an act as significant as intercourse.

Maybe you can relate to this bedroom scene. Your husband has already gone to bed. You assume he is asleep. Your baby has been fed and gently placed in the crib. Your own bed looks very comfortable, even though it hasn't been made up for several days. You crawl between the sheets, lay your weary head on your pillow, and close your eyes. You can't remember ever feeling so tired. There is not one ounce of energy left in your body. Then your husband's arm embraces you, and you know he wants to make love with you. Instead of responding to his embrace, you find yourself experiencing some resentment toward him, and there's a total lack of interest on your part.

This is a typical scene, and you have just reacted like many new mothers. Before too many days and nights go by, you and your husband must talk with each other and decide what kind of teamwork is necessary so you will be ready to share a mutual expression of love.

The circumstances that existed before the baby was born are no longer applicable. You don't have so much time to get prepared for an intimate rendezvous. There seems to be no time for a leisurely bath; the soft music doesn't harmonize with the baby's cries; your nightgown loses some of its effect when it's worn with a nursing bra; your last recollection of freshly cut flowers were those brought home from the hospital. (By the way, you may need to check. They might still be on a table somewhere because you haven't found time to dispose of them.) Total concentration is broken when you and your husband both know that at any given moment your intimate encounter may be interrupted by a baby who is not the least bit concerned with what is important to you.

In addition to the problems with outward surroundings, there are mothers who feel guilty because they cannot seem to give themselves fully to their husbands at this time. They feel as though they've neglected this area of marriage for several weeks, and now they don't want to disappoint their husbands.

Instead of anticipating this special time, women may also fear the possible physical pain involved. Other women find it difficult to relax during intercourse because of the possibility of another pregnancy. New mothers are vulnerable and highly sensitive to these thoughts, which are often byproducts of insufficient rest and the demands of a new role. These scenes and thoughts are real. They need to be dealt with successfully and effectively. Couples need to talk openly and find ways to continue their love life in a way that will bring satisfaction to both partners.

On a regular basis, you and your husband must decide how you, the mother and wife, can relax and detach yourself from your maternal role for a while. Recall things that relaxed you before the baby came . . . taking that unhurried bath, having a complete manicure, getting out of the house for a while, fixing yourself a cup of coffee or glass of iced tea and drinking it slowly, reading a magazine (but not about parenting), doing some relaxation exercises similar to those you learned during your childbirth classes, jogging or taking a walk.

Ideally, whatever you choose to do should be done while the baby is awake so that when you've had your brief recess from motherhood, you'll be ready to have an affair with your husband. The baby may cry while you're trying to relax, but, remember, your husband has volunteered to help with the baby, and he is in control of that situation.

As soon as your baby falls asleep, put your plans into action. It really doesn't matter about the time of day. No one has ever proven that you have to wait until evening for the most satisfying results. Learn to defy the ringing phone or doorbell. If you aren't interrupted, be grateful and make the most of the time you are able to spend with each other. If you are interrupted, try as graciously as possible to take a raincheck from your husband.

You and your husband will once again enjoy having intimate times with each other. Even with your stretch marks, sagging stomach muscles, and leaking breasts, he still loves you. He understands that you are busy, tired, and reluctant to dismiss the thought of the new baby from your mind. But if you will

,w it, your husband can briefly take you out of your busy, .emanding world. This is your special time together. Maybe in just a few minutes you'll need to share each other with the baby, but for now it's just the two of you.

The first few weeks after the birth of your baby, there will be days when you find it impossible to combine being a new mother with being a lover. You will learn to savor the times of being the lover you know you are. These times of intense planning in order to keep your love relationship growing will not last forever. They're just for *now.*

Reflections of a Wife . . . and Mother

In a short span of time both you and your husband have become absorbed with a new baby. It may be beneficial, therefore, for you to have some brief maternal intermissions. Take a few steps backward and observe the fragile attempts your husband makes at being involved in the baby's life.

If you pick up on your husband's desire to be involved, you're going to witness a miracle. He may discard a ritual that he's carefully developed ever since you've known him. He may actually choose to care for the baby instead of watching the evening news, sports, or any other television program.

Your husband will probably have some difficulty putting a diaper on the baby and making it stay on, but, just think, he's volunteered to do it. He won't hold the baby exactly the way you think he should, but watch how quiet the baby becomes in your husband's arms. You can't imagine your husband asking to bathe the baby, a baby who doesn't yet feel there is any profound merit to being bathed, but you have to admit that he does a relatively good, fast job.

You handle the baby daily which makes you a pro quickly. Your husband's physical contacts with the baby add up to only a few hours a day, so it'll take him longer to reach your child-care status. Yet he's a top shelf item with the baby. You can be grateful if you have a husband who wants to be a vital part of the baby's life as well as wanting to relieve you of some of your responsibilities.

It would be highly unrealistic for your husband to come home every day expecting to see a smiling and rested wife, holding a perfectly contented baby. For the first few weeks this is not the father's typical triumphal entry. There will be days when you will not have time to rest. The baby will not sleep, and you don't know why he won't sleep. The tension grows by the hour because you don't know what to do, and you're alone. You conjure up all kinds of things that might be wrong with the baby. Then you spend the rest of the day debating whether or not you should call the doctor. The fleeting thought of running away from home and baby may cross your mind.

Then your husband comes home. He's been at work all day, and he's missed being with you and the baby, and he's wondered how both of you have gotten along. It may be difficult for him to know how to meet your physical and emotional needs after one of your more trying, bewildering days. He'll probably be willing to find his niche in yours and the baby's needs, but be aware of his needs and the newness he feels in his role also.

(If your husband doesn't get overly enthusiastic reading books about babies, encourage him to at least read this next section. It is for him.)

Dear Husband,

I've recently discovered that there is no exclusive day set aside for mothers. Every day really is Mother's Day. Some days are better than others. I experience many exhilarating days in my new role, but some less satisfying ones sneak in with the good ones. These are the days when hardly anything seems to go right.

I've heard people say that all of us have the power built within us to do what needs to be done. This is not always true, especially when I'm floundering as a new mother. I feel like a fledgling trying to take care of a more helpless fledgling. I know I'll gain more finesse, but, right now, I grow so weary, and my weariness interferes with the enjoyment I thought I would have as a mother. Even knowing that someday soon I will grow more accustomed to our baby and to all the activities I've inherited does not soften some of my inner frustrations now.

For instance, on certain days things bother me that didn't used to bother me. Object: Husband. Examples: I don't like the way you throw your dirty socks by the clothes hamper instead of in it or the way you leave your shaving items, toothbrush, and toothpaste on the bathroom counter and your shoes in the middle of the room every day. You seem to be coming home later from work these days, and then you watch television when you finally do get here. It seems like you could see some of the things that need to be done without my having to tell you.

You've probably done all of these things since the day we came home from our honeymoon, but under my tired, critical eye all of your innocent acts are magnified and secretly resented. Why? Because your daily routines seem to be causing more work for me, and right now I don't feel like working any more overtime than I have to.

These frustrations of mine do not come because I've fallen out of love with you. They're negative thoughts that I've allowed to grow out of my fatigue, out of my new role for which no book or advice prepared me, and out of my desire to have some time for your companionship. I can't remember the last time we sat together and talked. Remember how we used to discuss things together after the evening meal? Remember how we used to lay in bed talking about what happened that day? We must take more advantage of these times. They're priceless to me because our times alone together are rare, and we can't allow ourselves to take them for granted anymore. We've got to be more sensitive to our own needs and not let our baby dominate our relationship.

You are the second member on this newly formed parental team, and I need you. I feel that I'm as successful at parenting as any other new mother right now, but I believe what I desperately need is your unreserved support. I've always needed it, but now that need is of a greater magnitude. Even though most of the time I feel I'm doing a great job, I need to hear someone say,

"You're doing a great job!" I'm quite sensitive right now. I guess it's because of my traumatic change in schedule and the revelation that I can't seem to detach myself from my awesome responsibility unless I feel some cooperation from you.

I understand you can't know what I need unless I tell you. You feel that I'm still the same woman you married, and I am, with one added attraction . . . a baby. I have some new needs that must be recognized and met.

Someday soon maybe I can tell you exactly what it means to me when you tell me that you want to take charge of the baby so I can get out of the house for a while . . . take a walk, go visit a neighbor, take a ride on my bike or in the car . . . get completely away. When I do any of these things, it's almost as though I've been granted a reprieve and found a freedom that I had taken for granted only a few short weeks ago. Then something strange happens after I've been gone for a while; I can hardly wait to get back home!

Some of my most simple pleasures, however, take place without leaving the house. When you tell me that I need a change of pace, I gladly take you up on it. I go to lie down and get perfectly quiet and relaxed because I know these times will be undisturbed; they're all mine. I might fix myself a warm bath and glory in your sensitivity to my need to relax. I make myself a hot drink and go into some realm of privacy to meditate on your goodness, our baby's life, our new family, and my personal needs of the moment. The sounds I hear from you and the baby are only mine to cherish. I have come out from these interludes strengthened, not only from the pauses themselves, but from my love for you which is strengthened because you have either seen or felt my need, and you've responded to it. That's my definition of *support.*

I love the way you initiate voluntary acts of love on your own: starting a load of clothes in the washer, trying to fold the baby's tiny clothes, vacuuming the house, picking up and putting away the daily accumulation of clutter, cleaning the table after a meal and washing the dishes. If I tell you how I feel it may seem as though I'm overreacting to something too simple to mention, and you may infer insincere appreciation or false flattery, but the truth is that you have voluntarily performed some unselfish acts, even when you, too, have had your own busy day at work. Each act has served as an exhibition of your support. That's exactly what I need now.

I've said that I also need to hear that I'm doing a good job as a mother, but I think it's time I thanked you for all you've done and are doing. You're doing a great job as a father! I want to thank you for not making a big deal out of sleeping in an unmade bed for five consecutive nights, for wearing the same unpressed shirt two days in a row, and for being patient as you tried to find two matching socks. Thank you for volunteering to run to the grocery store right before it closes to get something *I* forgot. Thank you for trying to be enthusiastic while blessing and eating the same leftovers for three different meals.

There has to be an award I could present to you for the miraculous insight you have at seeing my needs before I become aware of them, for laughing with me and for understanding my tears. I know I've been much too silent about expressing the happiness I receive just by knowing you want to be involved in our baby's life, but, believe me, it's a constant joy.

We've done a lot of growing up recently. We've had to detach ourselves from each other and our personal desires for a while, but strangely enough this detachment has transformed our relationship into a new beginning with each other. We don't have time to define it right now or fully understand how it'll affect our lives. For now it's satisfying to know that together we're becoming more accustomed to our new little boarder, and you and I are going to show this child how fortunate he is to be a part of our home.

I watch you as you hold our baby. I still can hardly believe that he is ours. Just think, a few short months ago we thought we knew, without question, what was important; but our values have shifted drastically during these last weeks.

I want to sit by you and have you put your arms around me.

In the brevity of this moment I want you to know that I love you and that you will always be important in my life . . . always!

Love,
Your wife

How I Feel About Today's Dads

I strongly agree with James Dobson's statement in his book *Straight Talk to Men and Their Wives.* He writes, "If American families are going to survive the incredible stresses of the 80's it will be because husbands and fathers begin to provide loving leadership within their homes, placing their wives and children at the highest level on their system of priorities."

A father's time away from his work can easily and innocently be consumed with meetings, church activities, civic organizations, and recreation. These things, as worthy as they are, devour a father's time with his wife and children. I believe that fathers are now taking a stand and are acknowledging a simple fact: their families need them, and they're going to do what has to be done to fulfill that need.

I can hardly wait to see how this generation is going to be affected now that the role of the father is being recognized and glorified. Men are beginning to realize that they are indispensable in the home. No one can be their substitute. They are at the core of family living. They are no longer spectators in their babies' lives; they are active participants. In a short time the world is going to feel the force of that active participation.

5

Equal Rights to Stay at Home

If someone were to say to you, "A woman's place is in the home," what would be your honest reaction? Would you feel smug because you have chosen to stay at home with your baby? Would you feel guilty because you have chosen to combine motherhood with another career, and you aren't sure if you have made the right decision? Would you be angry because no one has the right to tell you what you're to do?

Because of the changing times (*I think it's called progress*) and women's undefined roles at this time, the above statement could possibly launch a small-scale feminine World War III if taken at face value with no exceptions permitted. One group of mothers is emphatically in favor of staying at home full-time with their babies, committing themselves to twenty-four hour vigils of giving to and guiding these young lives. The other group of mothers cannot comprehend the credibility of full-time motherhood. There seems to be no middle ground, no plausible compromise on either side of this present-day dilemma.

I cannot defy progress, but I feel at liberty to recall how family life was a few short years ago. By comparing family life then with today's family lifestyles, I believe some of the values of the past will appear worthy of reconsideration.

There was a time when fathers were the sole providers for

their families. Evenings with the family were anticipated because Dad was at home after an eight-hour-a-day job. Mothers accepted the simple pleasures, the uncomplicated schedules, and the natural responsibilities their children brought them. There were clear-cut definitions of the maternal role. These women were the unacclaimed heroines, the quiet ones, the unpaid ones. They stayed out of the news media and picket lines. They were the ones who wore the apron. They were the home stabilizers. There is something to say about these moms who stayed at home. Perhaps they represented the steady force behind the truest meaning of "family."

Between those earlier days of family life and today's family scene something began to subtly invade this small social unit. Dad's job began to take more than eight hours a day to finish. Employers even began to take the liberty of sending dads away from home for days and weeks and sometimes months at a time. Society became more complex, and the phrase "for men only" was no longer relevant to the times. The men were no longer thought capable of running the affairs of the world alone. Mothers were encouraged to work outside the home. The words *prepared formulas, strained baby food,* and *disposable diapers* were introduced to the buying market. Because women began working outside the home, the words *day care* were also created.

These changing times, these new jobs, and these new words were possibly created as a result of the "All for Me" and the "Now" generations with little foresight as to how this new feminine work force would affect the future and security of the children. During these changes the value of the child, as well as the mother's role, has been placed in jeopardy.

Many of us are guilty of allowing this to happen. We have allowed an imbalance to occur. A new concept of parenting has surfaced and is being encouraged by people who speak, research, and write about the benefits of mothers working outside the home. The imbalance occurred when not nearly enough of us took the time to speak out, to share our experiences, and to write about the benefits of mothers who stay at home and who also continue to develop their lives, remaining useful by "just being a mother."

The phrase "just being a mother" means seeing our babies daily, guiding them, becoming acquainted with their needs, watching them grow. They see us, and they feel our special, personal, intimate touches, the kind of touches that computers can't register. We transmit a special love that is built in, and our babies receive it, regularly, daily, hourly. We are available to our babies when they are frightened by thunder, barking dogs, and strangers. We see their first smile and step. When we go somewhere, we usually take our babies with us. This satisfies our need for social contacts, and our babies realize they can be part of our pleasant experiences outside the home. No one can make us believe that there is a sufficient substitute for our personal day care.

I am highly in favor of mothers staying at home with their babies. But I am not so strongly biased that I am not aware of specific circumstances when a mother must work outside the home. Whatever the choice or circumstances, something needs to be clarified to all mothers. The words *staying at home* have a forever ring to them. I am not suggesting that a mother stay home forever and never consider another career or pick up the one she left at the birth of her baby. I am not suggesting she must stay at home until the last child turns into a young adult and walks out of the house to pursue a future apart from parents.

I do believe the time spent between the parent and the child at the beginning of every new life is highly significant. I will always believe this. The secular world has tried to make us believe that this contact isn't all that important. Yet, it is evident (some of the evidence being the breakdown of family life) that their secular ways don't always work either. Someone has written that if home life is suffering today, it could be because there has been a violation of its purpose.

It is the first three years of a child's life about which I'm most concerned. With strict discipline mothers, especially those who are career-oriented, can still continue to prepare themselves for future career goals during the years they are at home with their babies. Sooner than all of us are aware of it, babies are transformed into children who need their mother's care and attention less and less. Anyone who has researched the development of children knows that during the first several months babies are totally dependent on their parents, and the worth of those months together is immeasurable in importance. During those first fragile years everything babies are introduced to physically, socially, mentally, and spiritually is new. These areas, if developed properly, will come to be the whole person. Blessed are the parents who give the necessary time to make sure none of these areas are neglected.

Appropriate recognition and support must be given to mothers who are choosing to stay at home with their babies, letting them know the importance of what they are giving to the world and how they are honoring their role. Some of us must begin to upgrade the value of full-time motherhood.

Mothers who write "Occupation: homemaker" on insurance policies and medical forms must educate people to stop mentally visualizing women who have rips under their dress sleeves, safety pins on their blouses, hem lines held up with masking tape, flour on their faces, oversize fuzzy scuffs on their feet, and working vocabularies of ten one-syllable words . . . or less. Although these may very well be visible signs of early parenting, always remember that what *people* think or visualize isn't all that important. The Scripture says that we are to please *God* with our lives. I know of nothing that pleases God more than for Him to see women committing their days to being mothers, taking care of the basic needs of their children and loving them.

Much is being written about the experiences of today's working mother. This is good because conscientious mothers want to know how they can effectively manage their lives so they can spend necessary time before and after working hours with their children. There *are* assets included in a woman's decision to work, but I have noticed that little is being written for women who choose to stay at home. Therefore, this chapter is included to help stay-at-home mothers confirm that there is equal value in *their* decision.

How I Feel

The role of mothers requires an unlimited amount of unselfishness, and they receive only snatches of outside approval for what they're doing. The battle of whether to be a full-time or part-time mother starts when mothers find themselves living in a society that places little value on "just" rearing children. Society sees no conceivable way of measuring the worth of parenting when it bases both success and worth on a monetary scale.

In *Newsweek,* May 11, 1981, Grace Hechinger writes, "We've got to raise the scale again where we recognize our children as economic assets instead of economic burdens. We have this quality of needing to nurture and putting the needs for others ahead of ours and this is a direct opposite needed to make it in the outside/corporate world." Mothers have no tangible credentials. They are unpaid amateurs. Society has given them a low status rating, and the glory of motherhood has been handed over to, as Hechinger believes, "pediatricians, psychologists and social workers." This evidence causes a woman to feel that she has lost her purpose and her usefulness if she chooses to "just be a mother."

Mothers must not lose sight of the truth that the home is not an afterthought of creation. It is so vital to our earthly existence that it became the first social unit God established after He finished creating the world. "And the Lord God said, 'It isn't good for man to be alone; I will make a companion for him, a helper suited to his needs'" (Gen. 2:18, LB).

God knew that this social unit would play a significant rôle in the world. Every time a home is made secure, it branches out and affects all other social units. If the home unit, as small as it is, is a steady force, it triggers all other aspects of living. It is not secondary in God's plan; it is *first!* The blood relationships are so deep, so binding, so meaningful that there can be no substitute for what the home is intended to be.

Here are some basic truths as I see them. Families must be actively engaged in establishing strong home bases. Children are to be enjoyed; they have a definite place in our lives. Children must experience consistent love. Substitute parents cannot see the overall picture of our children's needs. Children need their parents. Parents are often pulled into demanding and selfish schedules that do not allow them time to think through and see that home life must take top priority, even if it isolates them for a while from the achievement-oriented world.

I believe there needs to be a briefing time to help parents see the significance of the early days after the birth of the baby. To be fair to all mothers I will say that I believe all conscientious mothers can have many of the same experiences with their babies whether they choose to stay at home or to work outside the home. But working moms must go the "second mile" in order to accomplish their goals. The rest of this chapter will discuss the value of the stay-at-home mother. The following chapter will pertain to the ones who decide to combine motherhood with a career.

Staying at Home

Sometime during the first six weeks when you are at home with your baby you begin to feel an unquenchable desire for some affirmation from the outside world. You worked at a job outside the home until your baby was born. You may have been in a position where you were recognized daily for your accomplishments. You were fully organized and made every minute of every day count. At the end of each day you could see the tangible results of your labors. You could measure your success by your visible productivity. All of this was minimized in importance when you made the decision to stay at home full-time after your baby was born. Now your decision stands before you in stark reality as you evaluate the first few weeks at home.

You lose sleep trying to answer the needs of your baby who seems only to cry, and you can only attempt to guess what to do. You've misplaced the definition of the word *schedule* and can only vaguely recall a time in your life when you lived through a routine day. There is evidence in every room that a baby is living in your house. Somewhere between sunrise and the late, late hours of nighttime, you squeeze in three meal preparations, wash one load of clothes but fail to transfer them to the dryer, and balance your baby on your knee while you talk on the phone. You must answer the phone. It might be your only contact with the adult world until your husband comes home. During these same days you try during three-minute breaks to continue some sort of relationship with your husband without bringing up the word *baby*. You fall quietly (so as not to wake the baby) into bed, demanding no more than three or four straight hours of sleep before the next feeding time.

It must be continually impressed on you that you are in the most lucrative business in the world. You're helping another human being get a positive start. You aren't receiving weekly paychecks with overtime for this work. The only person who sees how much energy you expend is your husband. The idea of reducing your world to you and your family for a while begins to diminish. Maybe you don't verbalize it, but you're silently questioning your worth as a mother. "If I'm so important, why am I not feeling important?" "I honestly don't feel appreciated for what I'm doing." "Couldn't someone else do as good a job as I am doing?"

This is where the briefing starts. In a period of a few weeks your baby has demoted you to a crude, uncomplicated way of living. All successful beginnings must start with basic needs being met. It's that simple . . . so simple it fails to imply the importance of its lifelong effects.

You need huge servings of positive reinforcement because your decision to stay at home is in complete opposition to the success-oriented culture to which you belong. You are now in the minority, and for some reason unknown to anyone, no one enjoys belonging to the minority. Mothers must learn to be different and to understand that sometimes the minority demonstrates the most strength. In this case it means ignoring the world's definition of success.

Being a mother is a career. It's a business. Its value is perpetual since it will be carried over into future generations. This business venture doesn't have office hours or a promise of a promotion. There are no guarantees of a "Mother of the Year" plaque, and you probably won't receive an engraved gold watch for faithful service. Being a mother is looking at a long-term situation in a present setting and grasping the value of "now."

Look at your baby. Concentrate on his features. It is difficult to imagine this approximately 21-inch being full grown. Your role is caring now, without seeing the end results. The faithfulness with which you carry out menial tasks every day is going to make an impact on your baby's life. You think they're too simple to be important? Not true. The faithful carrying out of the mother's role will be evidenced in the future. The molding of a new life begins instantaneously with birth. You have the unheralded privilege of minute-by-minute contact with your baby, transmitting love through your touch, your voice, your constant care, and the security that you provide with your presence. Are these things too bland to be fulfilling? To know that there is absolutely no other person on this earth who loves your baby as unreservedly as you do? In six short, action-filled weeks you have become your baby's

favorite blanket,
his (her) nightlight,
his soother.

You are his
connoisseur of strained baby food,
masseuse at bath times,
his lullaby.

You are his
first experience with love.

You are going to express love more beautifully, sincerely, untiringly, unselfishly than you ever have with any other living thing in your life. Because of all these generous acts, you will have introduced a lifetime of security to a being who will some day love as you have loved, who will face challenges as you have faced them. You will have had the time to say as well as to convey, "I will always love you."

You have not taken the easy way out of parenting by choosing to stay at home. It might be less complicated if you could punch a time clock, follow the routine of a job, close the door at 5:00, and head for home.

Staying at home has none of these outward compensations. It's demanding, unscheduled, unrecognized, and sometimes lonely. So, looking at this at face value, why should mothers opt to stay at home with their babies? You might consider your decision a sacrifice, but there is always a certain amount of sacrifice involved in doing what has lasting value.

Peter Marshall, in his book *Keepers of the Spring,* wrote, "The modern challenge of motherhood is the eternal challenge . . . that of being a godly woman. . . . We hear about . . . beautiful women, smart women, sophisticated women . . . but seldom do we hear of a godly woman. . . . I believe women come nearer fulfilling their God-given function in the home than anywhere else." One mother who chose to give up her career until her children were older said, "I am convinced more than ever that it takes a mother's full-time giving of love, encouragement and support even to come close to competing with what the world offers" (Bonnie Angel, "Decision," June 1980, p. 10).

Can You Be Fulfilled?

How do mothers, who sometimes give up successful careers, remain fulfilled persons by sticking to their decision to stay at home to "just be a mother"? First, you must attack and bring into submission the idea that fulfillment is wrapped up in self. Then, nix the belief that fulfillment has to do with what a person possesses materially or has the potential of possessing. These parallels will become extinct when mothers get back to the basic fact that babies have eternal worth. When this truth is acknowledged, mothers can totally devote their lives to their babies and to what they are preparing their children to give to the world. Then, long before you expect it, your baby will grow to a point where he will no longer need your constant care. It's at that time that you will experience complete freedom to fit back into the place you vacated before your baby entered your life.

Take apart the word *fulfilled.* "Full": Being wholly taken up with a thought or a plan (as with babies). "Fill": To put or pour into (as in your life's energies), to feed, a full supply (as in constantly, all, totally). The definition of *career* is closely associated with the word *fulfillment,* but in the sense we are using the word, it doesn't directly involve another person. "Career": "A course of continued progress in the life of a person." Being a mother could bring the same sense of fulfillment as a career because of all the progress that takes place, not only in the baby's life but also in the mother's life during those first years.

It may help you to know that your baby does not associate fulfillment with matching furniture, cloth napkins, designer jeans, or three-car garages. A baby doesn't see any of these things as status symbols. Because babies view the world from the lowly angle of a crib, their idea of fulfillment may seem illogical and sometimes futile when compared with the standards you've established. Their simple definition of fulfillment is to be supplied with their daily needs rather than future wants. So it is essential that you be continually reassured that you can be a fulfilled woman if you stay at home with your baby.

You're at Home . . . Now What?

You decide to stay home with your baby. When you come home from the hospital, within a matter of hours many changes start taking place. This new person is around the house twenty-four hours a day, and so are you. Both of you have to make many changes together. Your greatest adjustment is to stay at home when you've been programmed to get out of bed as soon as the alarm clock rings, eat a bowl of cereal, go through your morning routines, and rush out the door for work. Your baby's changes started when that small body was involuntarily expelled from a warm, soft, secure place to a world that psychologically would not always be warm and accepting and which would be filled with potential insecurities. Possibly you decided to stay at home when you realized the importance of making yourself available to attend to all of your baby's daily needs. With unequaled determination you wanted to make good things happen with and for your baby.

I cannot completely agree with the statement, "It's not the quantity of time you spend with your children, it's the quality time." I emphatically believe it's important to be consistently available to our babies even when it isn't convenient for us. These two beliefs are rivals. The first one was created during the "Self" era, the other one by those who are rebelling against the "All for Me" idea. We've begun to see the results of "The Self Age," and now are seeking to be a part of a bold new age.

Many of us feel strongly about parents being available to their children because we can personally remember the warm times created by our parents who were available to us and our needs. Many times our specific inner needs were not clearly defined, and being available didn't always mean that our parents were doing things with us. The security came because we knew our parents were close enough to respond if we called. Something unexplainable occurs when there are no visible signs of interaction taking place within a family group, but, at the same time, each person feels secure simply because everyone is there.

Even though our minds cannot recall many good feelings we had as babies, the value of our mother's presence was exposed as we became older. I can remember that my normal childhood accidents seemed less severe when Mother was there to pick me up and kiss away the hurts. The bad dreams went away more quickly when she came into my room and put her arms around me. The childhood diseases didn't bother as much because Mom was there with her special touch. The hurts I received from others diminished when Mother had the time to explain away the injustices.

Much of her participation in all my daily dramas was indirect, and yet, her influence continued to remain significant. I can only imagine that she was also there while I was a baby and security was in its earliest stages of development. All of this summed up says that when you choose to stay at home with your baby, your child will have constant access to your care. You'll be there. You'll be available. (The importance of this consistency will be discussed under the section on development of the emotional stability of your baby.)

You have the daily, unhurried privilege of creating special environments for and special moments with your baby. Some of your influence will be direct: feedings, cuddling, keeping baby dry and comfortable. Other times, you'll be concocting ideas to help your baby realize that this world has many benefits, the two main ones being your consistency in caring and your love.

Being at home will give you sufficient time to make some keen observations about your baby's total day. You'll read your baby's signals long before verbal communication begins. You'll quickly learn why your baby cries, how you can produce a happy smile, and what stimulation will produce a response. You are a most significant woman. You have the privilege, as well as the awesome task, of giving 100 percent of yourself to a tiny baby who can feel your love but hasn't yet recognized its value or how to openly respond to it. During the first busy weeks, keep in mind that you are nurturing every new sense your baby experiences. Learning is taking place although you see no evidence of it on your baby's sometimes expressionless face.

Many parents are anxious to know if they're doing all they're required to do as parents. The roles don't seem clearly defined. I do not have a simple solution, but I believe God has a guideline for parents to follow. In Luke 2:52 (RSV) the Scripture records, "Jesus increased in wisdom and in stature, and in favor with God and man." Jesus grew mentally, physically, spiritually, and socially. Doesn't it seem logical that if these were the areas in which Jesus developed, parents must be aware of the same development for their children?

Mental Development: The mental development is first established with the security parents provide for their baby. The Joint Commission on the Mental Health of Children believes that the earliest years of life are critical stages of development, and if, by chance, the mental development of the child is neglected or mishandled there could be irreversible damage. This committee has also observed that there are too many children who have sleep disorders, speech problems, bedwetting problems, and temper tantrams; children who are so dependent they cannot function properly; children who have prolonged periods of hyperactivity and a low tolerance toward any kind of frustration. Parents must realize that the emotional stability of their babies must be dealt with successfully. They must interpret their children's behavior in terms of its appropriateness or inappropriateness to their age and stage of development. Healthy emotional stability starts when parents surround their babies with security.

Research findings have shown that a baby's emotional stability is formed during early infancy. The love that babies receive from their mothers or mother substitutes from birth to three years will determine the path of emotional development that they will carry with them for the rest of their lives. To help create security in a child who is being groomed to live in an insecure world has to be one of the most important gifts parents can give their children. Dr. Lee Salk and Dr. Benjamin Spock strongly urge mothers to stay at home with their babies for the first three years. If the importance of this area of development is taken seriously, they believe it will insure sound emotional health.

Consider your part in the mental development of your baby. I believe that it is important for you to use your own unique way to establish security for your baby. Get to know, play with, and enjoy your child. You must take the initiative to provide your baby with stimulation and surroundings that will build intelligence and security.

Social Development: Be aware that your baby will need to know how to successfully interact socially. You must take time to introduce a wide range of social contacts. In the beginning you satisfy all your baby's social needs. Recognize the significance of holding your baby close to you when you feed, bathe, and talk to your little one. Cuddle, rock, and sing to your baby. After doing these things for several weeks, you'll see some social response. One day while changing a diaper, bathing, feeding, or talking, without any warning your baby is going to smile. You'll be so excited you might call your husband at work, and then you'll do anything you can to get another smile. You may wait a long time, but you've just witnessed your baby's first voluntary, social response. In all probability your faithful response to immediate needs helped create that smile. Smiles don't automatically happen. They form from appropriate experiences, and you get to take the credit for providing them.

Physical Development: The physical aspect of development may become mechanical, but that doesn't lessen its importance as you consistently take care of the physical needs of your baby . . . feeding when hungry, rocking when sleepy, and changing when wet for what seems like the tenth time in an hour. These methodical parent actions become more dramatic when you understand the value placed on the human body.

> Haven't you yet learned that your body is the home of the Holy Spirit God gave you, and that he lives within you? Your own body does not belong to you. For God has bought you with a great price. So use every part of your body to give glory back to God, because he owns it (I Cor. 6:19-20 LB).

Caring for the basic physical needs of your baby is as sacred as meeting needs in all the other areas of development. Each part of this new body is tiny and intricate, yet so significant and deserving of a good start.

Spiritual Development: Closely related to all three of these areas of growth is spiritual development. How do you introduce your baby to someone as great as God, our creator? Initially, your baby's first introduction to God's love is your love and care. So you see, all those endless, demanding, tiring jobs that you automatically acquired when you became a mother will not go unnoticed by your baby or by God.

Your baby indirectly encounters God through your love. Your baby needs to hear you pray even when too young to know there is such a thing as prayer. Pray for your little one by name. Pray before you feed your baby. Pray softly when you lay your sleepy one down at night. Show your baby the sunsets and explain that God made them. Quote Scriptures about God's love. Does all this seem foolish? Would you be embarrassed if someone saw or heard you do these things? You shouldn't. A person with eternal worth must be introduced to the One who created the world and who, in the process, created your baby to be a part of it.

The Family Plan

You may feel strongly about staying at home with your baby, but a gray cloud develops in your mind soon after you become pregnant or shortly after your baby is born. You cannot imagine how you can stay at home and still meet the family's financial demands with only one paycheck.

Ideally, it's good to make a trial run at living exclusively on your husband's salary a few months before your baby is born. Keep your paycheck in a "rainy day" savings account during the probation period.

Meeting your financial obligations is difficult if you have always budgeted with two paychecks. When you reduce the take-home pay from two paychecks to one, you'll immediately become aware of one obvious fact . . . you will have to completely change or modify your lifestyle. If you consider yourself a creative person, you can make this time in your life a game or challenge.

Maybe you never found it possible or even made an honest effort to set up a workable budget. You procrastinated because the word *budget* sounded too restrictive for your spending habits. The word *budget* may also make you visualize sitting at your desk for hours, plowing through endless paper work. It doesn't have to be that way.

The first prerequisite is for you and your husband to find a quiet time of day or night when both of you are rested and are determined to put your ideas on paper. You may want to spend several evenings or a weekend getting your plan ready for action. Remember at all times that nothing is impossible if you want to do it badly enough. As you start, have plenty of scrap paper to work out your figures. Repeat no less than once a day: "Ninety-five percent of the things we think we must have and can't live without are not necessary, and it will not end our existence if we can't have them."

The most obvious figure will be your actual take-home pay. Consider your monthly income and multiply it by twelve. Put this amount in large, bold figures at the top of your work sheet so you'll know exactly what you have to work with. Now break this amount up into weekly, biweekly, or monthly expenses, according to how often your husband gets paid. The two passwords at this point are DISCIPLINE and DETERMINATION. This will be a partnership arrangement. Look at each expenditure openly as you put it down on paper. Consider each other's feelings. Hang in there with your budget findings until you have them working for you. Then be ready to adjust your figures as your circumstances change.

There are some items that HAVE TO BE PAID. Other categories are necessary but can be modified. The important thing is how serious you are about living on a flexible budget in order to be able to fulfill your desire to stay at home with your baby.

Flexible Expenditures

Consider first the category we'll call "flexible expenditures"—the one where you'll be able to do the most trimming. As you trim these expenses remind each other that you won't be doing without anything, but you'll be modifying most everything. This may be difficult to carry through at first because you may have gotten into the habit of paying for conveniences. When you break this habit you'll automatically begin to reduce expenditures. You will naturally have to expand your mind to see how you can cut corners. All things considered, you're going to be the winner.

How to Use the Following Chart: Fill in the first two months of expenses by using information from your check stubs, bank statements, and receipts. Now begin to calmly discuss where you can start trimming. Do not lose your sense of humor. Things will be worked out eventually. Trim off the unnecessary fat. Discuss which categories each of you would be willing to cut down. Decide which categories you're definitely overspending. Each partner should do his own confessing, no prompting from the sidelines. Decide which things are important to you and which things can wait to be purchased.

Flexible Expenditures

Item	First Month	Second Month	Third Month	Fourth Month
Water				
Electricity				
Fuel				
Phone				
Medical				
Transportation (Auto Upkeep)				
Home Repair (Maintenance)				
Food				
Clothing				
Contributions/Tithe (Gifts)				
Entertaining				
Vacationing				
Hobbies				
Personal Care Items				
Unclassified personal (Dues, Books, Magazine subscriptions, Newspaper)				
Allowance				
Others				

How to Make Some of the Prime Cuts

Water: If you shower, get self wet, turn off water while lathering, then rinse. If tub bathing, do not fill tub to flood stage.

Electricity: Reduce unnecessary lighting. Use lower watt bulbs where possible. Be consistent and do not get aggravated when reminded to turn off lights when not in use.

Fuel: Check thermostat frequently. Wear heavier clothing in winter. If you have a fireplace, cut your own wood. Many farmers like to have their fence rows cleaned. That timber is usually the perfect size for fireplace wood. In summer, do not keep thermostat so low that frost appears on windows.

Phone: Use stationery and postage stamps rather than long distance calls.

Transportation: If you own two cars, use economically operated one most often. No backtracking when shopping. Car pool, ride bicycle, or walk when possible.

Auto upkeep: Study car manual. Lose your pride; do some of your own servicing . . . rotate tires, change oil (buy oil on sale), wash your own car.

Home repair: Books are available to show you how to do your own repairs including interior and exterior work such as masonry, painting, paper hanging, plumbing, heating and electrical work. This is not only a savings but can be most rewarding.

Food: Prepare meals that will make second meals in leftover form. Go to grocery store once a week (unless you have unexpected company). Make list before going shopping. Plan weekly menus. Keep a paper on kitchen counter and add to your list throughout the week as you run out of certain food items. Use lesser cuts of meat, have meatless meals, collect and use coupons, watch for specials, brown-bag it for work, avoid convenience foods, freeze leftovers and don't forget to use later, create casseroles with leftovers. Eureka! A new recipe.

Clothing: Be aware of garage sales, shop at secondhand stores, make your own clothing, coordinate outfits, buy at out-of-season sales.

Contributions: Go in with others to buy nicer wedding, baby, and anniversary gifts. Keep gifts at a minimum. Set a price and stick with it. Give only to the charities that you feel strongly about.

Entertaining: Have carry-in meals, glorified casseroles, desserts only; each guest bring an item to put together, e.g., banana splits, tacos, submarine sandwiches. Take advantage of free community services: concerts, parks, libraries, lectures, recreation centers, art exhibits, museums.

Vacationing: Get better acquainted with your state. Plan less extravagant trips. Have you tried camping? While traveling be aware that meals served in restaurants at noon are always less expensive than evening meals. Buy fruits and cheeses for evening meals.

Hobbies: Finish one project at a time. Save change until you get enough money to buy additional craft supplies.

Personal care items: Buy on sale; use cut-rate drug stores; buy in volume when prices are lower.

Unclassified personal: *Dues:* Drop membership in clubs not really interested in belonging to. *Magazines:* Cancel subscriptions to magazines and newspapers you never get around to reading.

Allowance: Come up with an agreeable amount for each other. The way of spending should be unaccounted for. This will give each of you a sense of freedom . . . not locked in.

I used a foolproof way to stay within my weekly expenditures when my children were small and we were living off one paycheck. I wrote one weekly check (I still do). It included money for groceries, gas, school lunches, allowances, etc. When I cashed the check, I asked for specific denominations. Each amount allotted was put into a separate envelope. If there was any money left in any envelope at the end of each week, I put it back into my secret corner. When I had saved enough for a particular item I wanted, I purchased it. I don't know how many times I could've been laughed or kidded out of my game, but I loved it.

Fixed Items

Again, use check stubs, bank statements, and receipts to fill in the following. Changes to consider: Insurance: compare with

Fixed Items (Costs for a year)

Item	First Month	Second Month	Third Month	Fourth Month
TAXES				
Federal				
State				
Property				
Auto				
INSURANCE				
Medical				
Life				
Property				
Auto				
DEBT PAYMENTS				
House (or rent)				
Auto				
Others				
SAVINGS				
Vacation				
Major appliance replacements				
Christmas spending				
Furnishings				

other insurance companies to see if you can get the same coverage for less. Move to a less expensive house (unheard of?). Get by with one car or a smaller, more economical one.

You may not consider "savings" a fixed item, therefore, you may be tempted not to put this category in your budget. Start saving 1 percent of your monthly income. This is not a fine you pay; it's a gift you give yourself. It's a systematic way to reach your goals. Learn to do with lesser items in order to buy items that will bring greater satisfaction.

After you subtract the total expenses from the total amount of your income and you find that you have some money left over, gently transfer any remaining amount toward your savings or another form of investment. The more often your savings is compounded, the more this slot will expand.

As you begin your trial run be bold, unashamed, proud at telling each other how you are saving in particular areas. After two months add up your expenditures and put your findings in months three and four. Compare these columns with the columns for the first two months.

Notice whether you are spending differently from your plan. See if you bought something you hadn't planned to buy. Did you fail to keep a record of some of your spending? If you've had trouble sticking to your plan, write down the words "More Discipline." Take a mental picture of those two words and carry them around in your mind for another month.

You may need to rework your budget from time to time. There's nothing wrong with that. You're to be commended for facing a problem and seeking a solution. The beauty of this whole family plan is to prove to yourself that you can stay at home with your baby.

Mothers Who Have Done It

Mothers have varying reasons for choosing to stay at home with their babies. They become willing to change their lifestyle for a while, and they commit themselves to total mothering, many still not completely understanding the full implications of it. Yet, even on the days they feel that it would be easier to have a job outside their homes, the future rewards of parenting still outweigh the present desire to continue another career. One mother shared that when she became pregnant she made the decision to stay at home after her baby was born. "My family had to come first, and knowing myself the way I do, I knew I would have to make some sacrifices. I didn't want one of those sacrifices to be my family."

When mothers see how quickly their babies change, within a matter of days the decision to stay at home firms up. Mothers have a built-in maternal instinct that urges them to be there in the reserved section to see daily miracles occurring. A first-time mother said, "Some places in my house are just going to have to go unattended because I don't plan to miss out on a thing in my daughter's development. I want to be there, and I want to see the first time my baby does something new. It might lose its significance when I get it secondhand."

Mothers who spend their days with their babies have a way of tuning in to their baby's signals. They want their baby's training to come from them. They want to be the caretakers. They agree with others who believe that the consistent caring, the sameness of routine, the being there when it's happening confirms the rightness of their decision to stay at home.

The Second-Mile Mom

There is a special group of mothers in today's world. They're the second-mile moms, the ones who are working outside their homes. Are you one of those women who has decided to combine motherhood with a job? Have you assured yourself or been assured by others that you can be an effective mother *and* work outside the home? Your decision to work doesn't keep you from experiencing the same things mothers who stay at home experience. You'll also have those special times with your baby, encouraging growth, watching development, creating and enjoying times with each other. You just have to commit yourself to go that second mile with your baby before and after working hours. You too get tired, physically and emotionally. You have days when nothing seems to go right, when others make too many demands on you; you wonder if you're a good mother. You share something in common with the mothers who stay at home; both of you love your babies. You want to give them your best.

Some mothers are not given the option of staying at home. They have to go back to work. Isolated circumstances force some mothers to go back to work as early as six weeks after the birth of their babies. The decision to return to work so soon is probably not their choice and might seem unfair to them but is necessary in order to meet outstanding financial obligations.

If you fall into the category of the working mother I hope this chapter will offer encouragement to you, even if you must leave your baby at such an early age. I want you to see that you can still have satisfying and rewarding years as a mother. If you've made your decision to go back to work and you still do not feel good about leaving your baby, study the budget proposal in Chapter V. It might enable you to stay at home with your baby at least awhile longer. You might also receive help by ordering the book, *Catalyst,* 14 East 60th Street, New York, NY 10022. This book lists jobs for mothers who would like workshifts that accommodate their parental duties. I believe this will become a future service for mothers who are competent in their work and must work to supplement the family income, yet who feel strongly about staying home during their children's formative years.

There are other women who, even though they do not have to work, enjoy working outside the home and feel that they can comfortably combine both roles. This group feels that they are stronger in their maternal role because they have some time away from their children. Many of these women take part-time jobs during their children's first few years since they feel they are not quite ready to be absent from them for long periods at a time.

There is another group of women who are highly trained in professional skills which make many of us richer by their contributions. They believe strongly enough in the results of their work that they are willing to organize and make the best of both roles. They have a sense of independence that must be satisfied, and the only way this can happen is by continuing their careers.

Working mothers don't show less love for their children because they choose to work outside their homes. Being a mother is an accomplishment in itself, but there is also a deep drive within certain women that causes them to want to combine other accomplishments with motherhood. With this determination, both roles can fuse together successfully.

The main sacrifice I see working mothers make is to give up or not become so deeply involved in other outside interests, especially during their first years of parenting. This area of personal development can't be discarded. It stands to reason, however, that when a mother is gone from her child all day, she wants to assume the second of her dual roles after working hours; therefore, little time is left to participate in other social activities. This is where she will have to serve herself an extra portion of unselfishness.

Although a job is important to you either because of the needed extra income or simply because of the satisfaction it brings, keep in mind that although a job is worthy of both your time and intellect it is no longer the top-shelf item in your life. The priority of your job shifts to second place with the birth of your baby. As long as a working mother can keep this perspective, the role of parenting will certainly not be neglected.

Motto: Get Organized

When you go back to work, you are immediately confronted with the need to organize. If you diligently work at organizing, you will soon gain recognition as the queen of fast food deliveries and one-day washing and cleaning services, and you'll probably be recognized as the most agile aisle-hopper in grocery and department stores.

There is now more to consider before leaping into your car and heading for work each day. You have someone else to consider, a little one who will not comprehend the urgency of Mother getting to work on time, fully dressed and composed. So organization becomes inevitable. Included in your daily schedule should be allowances for the unexpected. A word of caution to the highly organized woman: keep your organization flexible enough so that you won't feel trapped when the unexpected occurs. A rigid schedule could add stress to your already busy life.

To make your planning work for you, it will be mandatory that you stand in front of your mirror every day and practice shaping your mouth to say the word no. You are young, creative, ambitious, and vulnerable to feeling useful and needed. Plus, until your baby was born, you had the reputation for being able to get things done well. People recognize your kinds of energies. After all, social organizations run more smoothly with a woman like you on their team. When you're tempted to say yes only because of the honor, prestige, or recognition, an instant flashback of your baby's face as well as of your family's needs may help. Then you'll be able to say firmly but graciously, "No, the construction of my home is now in progress . . . maybe later."

You can't say no to everything, but at least learn to say no to those things that you feel will not benefit you, the things you participate in for the simple reason that "I always have." The organization, if it's worthwhile at all, will still be in existence in a few years, while the needs of your baby won't. Saying no will not be forever, just for now.

Practicing the art of saying no is high on the agenda of working mothers. This is not a selfish act on your part. It simply means that you've seen the value of giving prime time to your family before and after working hours. I believe you will want to devote most of your evenings, especially through the week, to your family. You don't have to make apologies to anyone for doing this. This family commitment will give you unrushed times for playing, cuddling, and laughing together. You will not have to rush the end of the day. You will have the time to create the warm atmosphere that you, your husband, and your baby will need to recall while all of you are away from each other the next day. These good times together will be valued by your family.

Your husband plays a significant role in your being a second miler. The two main considerations are shared responsibilities and mutual support. Neither of you will have totally separate lists of responsibilities. You will simply help each other as each need arises. Draw up an unwritten contract which states that you and your mate will talk situations out as they present themselves so you won't drain your energies feeling that one or the other is not making the team effort or is making the support system unstable.

It does take team effort to keep the house relatively straight;

the clothes sorted, washed, folded, and put away; the diaper bag loaded; the meals prepared; the groceries bought; the gas tank filled; the bills paid; the lawn sprinkled, mowed, and raked; the snow shoveled; the plumbing repaired. Some of these categories require masculine strength, others, feminine insights. But there are times when both of you will be called on to cross over into the other's line of responsibility . . . anything to bring about positive solutions to the many daily tasks you face when you're both working toward the goal of creating times to interact as a family.

Agree that major decisions and trivial disagreements will not be discussed when both of you have had an unusually trying day at work. Silence at this point may be more healing than talking.

You and your husband are exceptional. Both of you are going the second mile. You are forcing two roles to work. You may feel that you are making sacrifices, and you will; but you're doing it in order to have sufficient time together as a family. Common sense tells you that moderation is healthy under any circumstances. This includes moderating your life in order to have adequate time with your family as well as having time to continue particular outside interests that will benefit both of you. Since every family situation is unique, you must decide how to balance each area without the neglect of the others.

Choosing a Caregiver

You have made the decision to go back to work after your baby is born. You will now want to scout around to find the best caregiver possible for your child. As you begin your search, pray for guidance to find that special one who will care for your child. When you leave for work each day you will want to be sure your baby is going to receive the best at the hands of a loving person. You may want a caregiver who has a philosophy of child care similar to yours, and who believes in the worth of the young life placed in her care.

General characteristics of a dedicated, effective caregiver include: past experience in dealing with children, a genuine love of children, a cheerful disposition, a primary concern for the child and not particular television programs, patience during trying situations, consciousness of your child's physical and emotional needs, and desire to give 100 percent of herself not only for the child's good but also for your comfort while you're away from your baby. This type of person values her job as highly as you value yours.

It is rare to find a person who is willing to come into your home, but it certainly isn't an impossibility. Almost as ideal, but not as convenient, is locating a person with these qualifications who is willing to care for your baby in her home.

This kind of person will not run an ad in the newspaper or put a poster in store windows or on public bulletin boards, but this kind of person does exist. Many mothers look within their churches, or at least contact the church office to see if staff members know of someone who would be interested in caring for children. Names can also be obtained from other mothers who know of persons with outstanding qualifications.

Another possible solution is to have a relative who volunteers (no arm twisting) to care for your baby. There's no doubt that this person will see that your child's needs are met. One mother shared how her mother keeps her son. She said that her mother follows many of the same Christian principles that she does about child rearing. This arrangement also gives the child the rich experience of being loved daily by Grandma. In a case like this communication lines between mother and daughter must remain open so that misunderstandings don't have room to materialize, especially in the areas of discipline, eating, and sleeping habits.

Until your caregiver becomes familiar with daily routines, you will be her basic source of information and, without sounding too militant, her authority. She will need to know the following in order to give the best care: your business and doctor's office phone numbers, written directions about when and what to feed, bedtime information, and other general schedules for the day. Interspersed throughout each response to your baby's basic needs will be the extra amount of love and affection she gives to your child. You will know you have made an excellent choice when you open the door after a tiring day at work and are met by a relatively straightened house . . . the result of your caregiver having the foresight to go the second mile in her job.

You may not succeed at locating someone who will care for your child on a one-to-one basis, so you may need to consider an independent caregiver who watches several children in her home. As you think about this possibility, be aware that the larger the group of children, the less individual attention your child will receive. This may not be a problem with you. Your decision to put your child in this type of situation will hinge on the value you place on your child receiving personalized care.

The key to look for in an independent caregiver who keeps several children is her desire to provide a home-away-from-home atmosphere. She will probably be a woman who has enjoyed rearing her own children and continues to find satisfaction in her maternal role by caring for the children of others. She will be a natural when it comes to caring for and loving children. Because of her commitment (it has to be commitment because her fees are extremely nominal), she plans her day around the children's needs. Because your child's needs are being met, you can feel at ease when you place your child in the waiting arms of this faithful caregiver and then leave to devote yourself to a day at work. This is one of many reasons it's important to find the best caregiver available.

What options do you have when you aren't successful at finding any of these home or away from home child-care solutions? You may need to look into the possibility of placing your child in a day-care situation. But where do you start?

The preliminary search may start by talking with your pediatrician to get some plausible ideas. You may want to contact other mothers who are leaving their children in day-care centers. If you are in a city that provides a local public agency responsible for child care, call them and get a list of licensed facilities in your area.

You may need to seriously consider the location of the day-care facility and decide how much time you are prepared to spend traveling. The effectiveness of the day care is top priority, but the location must also fit into your work schedule.

As you visit different facilities, make out a list of questions to be answered by those managing the day-care centers. Some of these may be high on your list of priorities; others may not fit your specific situation.

Approach to day care: Is the function of the day care strictly organized on a professional scale, or is it family oriented . . . high on compassion, stimulation, and flexibility?

Policies: How do they work at helping the child adjust to the new situation? What is their procedure when the child gets sick or is involved in an accident?

Feeding procedures: If your child is older, ask if the food served will provide one-third of daily nutritional needs and also whether nutritional snacks are served each morning and afternoon. (Some day-care centers also provide weekly menus so that parents won't duplicate the meals.)

Expected fees: Is the cost of their services clear to you?

Insurance: Do they have a comprehensive general liability policy with a so-called premises medical payment endorsement?

Developmental areas: Will your baby be restricted to a playpen or will activities be planned to help your child explore an expanding social world, as well as creating atmospheres for emotional development and creative play?

Licensed: Have they been properly evaluated and licensed to meet the highest standards of care?

Progress report: Will there be a daily report on your child's activities? For example, how much your child ate, slept, what educational activities were introduced, and how your child responded to those activities.

You'll also appreciate the day-care centers that encourage you to visit. Otherwise, the center's personnel may feel that they are taking over the rearing of your child, and no conscientious day-care person wants that total responsibility.

When you narrow your choices down to one or two facilities, it is important that you visit them and stay approximately one-half hour at each. Mornings are usually the best time because the children are active. Then drop in unexpectedly in the afternoon to see how things are going when everyone is tired.

After you have made your final decision concerning a caregiver, have an alternate plan in mind for any given day. Your ideal plan may not always be in working condition. The usual time for the alternate plan to be set into motion is when your child or your caregiver becomes ill. Don't count on sickness occurring only on weekends, holidays, or your days off. Have a substitute sitter on call. If this is not dealt with at the start, you could be setting yourself up for some days of tense beginnings.

Is It Worth It?

You've experienced many changes in your life since your baby came. One of those changes occurred when you went back to work. Many mothers can make this adjustment with little effort; others find it extremely difficult. The first group feels comfortable about leaving their babies in the care of someone else during their workdays. The latter group has guilt served with their meals, takes it to bed with them, and carries it around before, during, and after working hours.

What is the difference between these two groups of second-mile moms? There's a large difference between the woman who feels that she is contributing to society's needs with what she is doing in her profession and the woman who is forced into a "have to" working situation that she doesn't particularly like. This woman works only because she has to help meet financial obligations, and all the while she wants to be at home with her baby. These mothers must constantly try to maintain a positive attitude about their situation because their attitude will be transmitted to their babies and will ultimately determine their success at combining parenting with working.

Years ago I met a conscientious Christian mother whose husband was finishing his college degree. She didn't have a choice. She had to work. She shared with me that she felt guilty about leaving her baby, but there was no option for her. I remember assuring her that if there was no possible way for her to stay at home, then I felt that God, in His wisdom, would provide for her baby's needs while they were away from each other. I still contend that I was right in my statement to her.

Many mothers feel guilty about working, but guilt only drains the energies a mother needs for effective parenting, which draws on all available human emotional energies. Guilt is a negative aspect of life that must be recognized, dealt with, and discarded daily. How can it be handled, especially in the lives of the mothers who must work? It isn't easy, but there are some solutions.

If you're one of those mothers who feels guilty about working, call time out some evening or weekend when you and your husband do not feel rushed, both of you are relatively rested, and your baby has had a good day. With all this going in your favor, you will be able to deal more positively with the feelings of guilt that have been plaguing you since you went back to work.

An excellent guide to study during this evaluation time is *Help: A Handbook for Working Mothers* by Barbara Greenleaf with Lewis A. Shaffer, M.D. The author helps mothers recognize symptoms of stress and shows how to reduce them and resolve them. She shows how you can manage your household more effectively and how you can build a strong family unit in the limited amount of time you spend together. If this book cannot be obtained at a bookstore or at a public library, there are other excellent books available on this subject.

Do some self analyzing. Ask the big questions first. "Why am I feeling guilty?" "Am I justified in feeling this way?" Take all the time you need to answer these questions. The answers may solve the majority of your problems. In two columns write down the positive and negative aspects of working. Verbalize these to your husband. He may be able to see some of the factors more objectively than you, so consider his insights and write them down with yours.

Together decide if the support system between the two of you has weakened, perhaps because you feel most of the responsibilities have shifted to your side. Both of you may need to seriously consider eliminating some of your extracurricular activities for a while in order to get a better balance established between the two of you.

It is so important to keep the support system working because the days that give parents the most problems are those days when the unexpected occurs. Baby starts the day earlier than usual, earlier than you want to start. Baby wakes up cross for no particular reason and that irritability subtly invades both of you; you find yourselves becoming irritable, also. The most simple annoyances . . . alarm didn't go off, no clean diapers, no milk for breakfast, shirt needs ironing, snow during the night, baby's clothes didn't get dry . . . will be magnified. They have the potential of igniting because two tired parents teamed with one cross baby will find it impossible to figure out even the most simple solutions to the most simple problems at the start of a busy day. At this point nothing looks right because both of you are weary of trying to make everything synchronize with your work schedules. To further complicate matters you begin to feel guilty and fantasize, "This wouldn't be happening if I didn't have to work." This is an unrealistic thought because mothers who do not work outside their homes experience some of the same explosive, behind-the-door scenes. These days are going to happen. Facing this fact, you and your husband work to keep a flexible support system functioning. You'll know you have succeeded when some situations get so ridiculous that you have a sudden urge to laugh . . . and you do, right in the middle of chaos.

Here are some other positive, concrete ideas to consider. If you feel they will help you . . . do them. You're worth it! Plan to eat out once a week . . . just you and your husband. Yes, you leave your baby each day while you work, and it costs extra to eat out and get a baby-sitter; but a quiet, inexpensive meal that probably won't last more than an hour can relieve your fatigue, revive your outlook on life, and create new incentives for you as a wife, mother, and career person.

Also, somewhere in your neighborhood there lurks a competent high-school student who is willing to do anything for extra income, even clean your house. It may take that person only two or three hours per week to take care of particular household chores you feel need to be done, but which you can't seem to get done. Having help in this area will create more time for you to spend with your baby, thus relieving much of your guilt. Decide on the amount you can pay this person, and then together work out the hours. Another thing you may need to develop in order to enjoy the time you do have with your baby is the ability to walk into your house after work, pick up your baby, mentally resign from your job, and totally enter into your domestic career.

If, after diligently trying to combine working with parenting, you still do not feel good about it, you may want to approach your employer about working part-time. If you are efficient, reliable, or possibly indispensable, you may be pleasantly surprised when he takes you up on your offer. If not, you may want to make a complete change to a regular part-time job. Naturally, this decision will reduce your income. Yet if it reduces the frustration and guilt you experience when leaving your baby for long periods of time, you'll find ways to compensate for the financial loss.

Your Decision

> Research has shown that mother's employment doesn't, in itself, adversely affect children. Much depends on the mother's attitude and the quality of the care the child receives from her as well as other caregivers. Most people now believe that an employed mother can have as good a relationship with her children as a mother who does not work outside the home (Joseph H. Pleck, Program Director of the Family Program at Wellesley College Center for Research on Women, New-Leader, Sunday, November 30, 1980).

It was so simple when you were single and were responsible only for yourself. The day you married you committed your life to another life: enter responsibility number two. You and your husband committed your lives to caring for a baby: enter responsibility number three. With each responsibility comes changes and new roles. For some mothers, responsibility number three has caused them to make one more significant choice. "Shall I continue my career, or shall I devote the next several years of my life as a full-time mom?"

Some of you hope that someone else will tell you which decision is best for you and your baby. But that someone is not qualified to make that choice for you. As long as your husband, your child, and you are top priorities with your job coming second in importance, you will be satisfied with and effective in your dual role.

I loved and cared for my children in my way. There was no conflict. If I could have the privilege of being a mother to small children again, I would make the same choice. I want the same for you. Your satisfaction and mine comes from knowing, no matter what decision we make, we are attempting to do the best we possibly can in rearing our children.

7

How Babies Change Lives

Do you enjoy being a mother? Have there been days when you wished you weren't one? A young mother who had an exceptionally frustrating day with her sleepless, fretful four-month-old daughter told her husband, "I don't think I want to be a mother anymore." He replied, "I don't believe that's the way it works!"

Question: Why would any mother have a thought like that? Answer: It's a reasonable thought after a particularly bad day. There are days when your baby is inconvenient, uncooperative, and an intrusion on your privacy. Babies have the natural ability to change your plans, routines, expectations . . . your life.

This thought of not wanting to be a mother anymore usually occurs on the days when you aren't sure if what you're doing really has much lasting significance. You may also desperately need to hear someone commend you for what you're doing.

But balanced with these questionable days are the other days when your baby takes long naps, contentedly lies in the crib, sleeps through the night, doesn't spit out the strained baby food. These are the magnificent days when you get to both shampoo and condition your hair, you have time to take a nap, and you get the evening meal completely prepared without any interruptions. Besides that, you get to eat what you've prepared while the food is still warm. On these favored, long-deserved days your mind clears. You begin to revel in the truth that you have the privilege of being a mother whether or not it's in complete harmony with your life's desires. These are the days when you're reminded that time for yourself has not been totally deleted from your life.

What's a Parent to Do?

"Life is worth nothing unless I use it for doing the work assigned me by the Lord Jesus" (Acts 20:24, LB). This verse should make any question you have about parenting obvious. You've been given a twofold assignment by God. That assignment is to have sufficient time to care for your baby's needs and your own needs. This isn't difficult to accomplish during the first few weeks after your baby's birth because people realize your time is being consumed as a new mother. You need more rest, so it's a time when others hesitate to ask you to do any more than you're already doing.

After a few more weeks, however, these same people begin to contact you to ask you if you'd be willing to get involved in particular outside activities. Maybe you'll feel like doing them, and maybe you won't. You are the only one who will be able to judge fairly what you're capable of performing in addition to being a mother. But here's the way some mothers' minds work. "I AM feeling stronger; the baby is doing well. I've begun to feel a little guilty for not doing something other than caring for my family." Before you are completely aware of what has happened, you have become the prime candidate for every club office vacancy and door-to-door collector for every legitimate benefit drive in town.

You do need diversions from being a mother, but those diversions must meet *your* immediate and specific needs. It is not selfish to do only those things that will enhance your effectiveness as a mother. You may need to be made aware of a basic spiritual truth to help you decide what you're to do.

In the first chapter of the Book of Ephesians the apostle Paul explains what God did to bring about His plan for eternal life for all people. In verse twelve he summarizes by writing, "God's purpose in this was that we should praise God and give glory to him for doing these mighty things for us" (LB). Notice the words "praise" and "glory." Praise is having time to compliment God, to express how much you love Him for who He is and for what He has done and is doing. To give "glory" is to do things with your life that will make God happy. These two things are lifetime requirements for all Christians.

Think of this verse in light of your role as a mother. At this time, there is nothing more useful, fulfilling, or sacred than caring for your baby and yourself in a way that will please God. These are the two basics with which you are to concern yourself. If you deviate from these, you will begin to complicate your life with so many other things that you will not have the time to be the mother you know you can be. By being aware of these basic truths you will be able to discern between what people are asking of you and what God is asking of you.

You are living in a world whose only pace is fast. Its values are full of contradictions, and the worth of what you're doing as a mother is downplayed. Many people do not see the significance of parenting as you do. They are unaware that doing additional things right now might jeopardize the goals you have set for yourself. Since you will always be faced with outside demands, you must set up your own standards and your own pace in order to have the time you need to be an effective parent.

The following exercise may give you a fresh insight into parenting and could remain in effect until your full-time years of motherhood are completed.

A time to think: In your mind, visualize your house. What does it look like? Is it frame or brick? Think about a specific room in your house . . . the arrangement of the unmatched furniture, the curtains. What does your car look like? Color? How many more payments until it's yours? Does it need cleaning? How about your clothes? Think of a favorite outfit. Why is it your favorite?

Now think about your husband. How about his physical features, a special time you've enjoyed together, things he has done that have made you happy or proud?

Think about your baby, how you anticipate the birth, the day of the actual birth, the changes your baby has brought, the dreams you have, the dreams that have already come true.

At the beginning of the exercise you thought of things that God allowed people to make. As a Christian you know that there will come a point in time when all of those things will no longer exist.

God created, firsthand, your husband, your baby . . . you. These are absolutely the only parts of His creation that will last forever . . . eternally.

When you commit yourself to caring for other human beings who have eternal value, it's worth every moment you spend involved in your family's lives. Something this significant must not be downgraded by a society that does not recognize or comprehend the eternal worth of the people who make up that society.

Becoming a Mother

Have you ever been busier than you are now? Did the baby books you read fail to inform you properly about what was included in a woman's life when she became a mother?

You've already found out that babies, especially yours, often defy the rule of thumb about eating, sleeping, and crying. Because there's no chapter in any book that adequately describes what you're experiencing, you begin to rely on your own native common sense and decide completely on your own how you're going to fit into your new role. It all has to do with "becoming" . . . learning as you go. You don't comprehend all there is to know about mothering as soon as you hold your baby the first time, but everything that happens from that moment is going to have a lasting effect on your life. It all depends on how you react to situations . . . situations for which books, doctors, family, and friends cannot adequately prepare you. No one is intentionally trying to keep anything from you; it's just that they know with firsthand experiences will come firsthand wisdom and knowledge.

On your own you will learn to laugh when you've put the last clean diaper on your baby, when you've crawled all through the house and still can't find a pacifier, when you've laid down to rest and the baby wakes up; when you burn supper for the third evening in a row. You'll question whether you will ever experience the ecstasy of another good night's sleep, get your body back into its original shape, or if your stretch marks will ever fade.

You'll panic when the baby-sitter cancels at the last minute or when your baby starts to run a high fever late at night. You'll pray for strength and receive answers to your requests.

You'll cry when you can't explain why you're crying. You'll just know it's the only alternative at the moment that makes you feel better. You will learn not to feel guilty for walking away from parenting for a while so you can have some time to yourself. In that time you will think and discover the right combination of self-sacrifice and selfishness, recreate the image of your own personhood, and gain confidence in yourself as a new parent. At other times you'll visit with other young mothers . . . laughing, crying, sharing, comparing, and supporting each other.

You'll have precious moments when you'll sit by your husband with his arm securely around you. You'll hear him say, "You're doing a great job, Mom." You'll tell him unashamedly that you're tired of all the daily demands, that you need to get away from the mothering role . . . and he'll understand.

You'll hold your baby close so that you'll feel that warm, receptive little body next to yours. You'll determine in that special moment to keep your life simple in order to have time to look at your baby and marvel at this little person's existence.

"You're Not Going to Believe This!"

You are at a time in your life when you can't possibly see an end to the activities and responsibilities that go with being a parent. You are deeply involved with "now." You may wonder through the years if this constant involvement will ever end.

Ask any mother who is now sitting in her empty nest, and she will tell you that there will come a time when you will get to sleep undisturbed through an entire night. You will use the worn out diapers for cloths to wipe the dust off your unmatched furniture, trimmed in Early Teeth Prints. You will revive the lost art of doing the washing only once a week and marvel at having peanut-butter-and-jelly-free walls and doorknobs. You will walk across the kitchen floor, and you won't stick or crunch.

You will remember the wonder that was in your child's eyes when taking the first step, walking in the grass barefoot, seeing snow and rain the first time, touching a puppy, holding a baby rabbit.

The years will come when you will no longer show your children how to tie their shoes, look both ways before crossing the street, get cats and kites out of trees, balance bicycles, throw a ball, create tunnels and castles out of sand. You'll wonder who taught your children how to catch lightning bugs and put them in jars, how to put dirt on slides so they could slide faster, how to balance on a teeter-totter, how to make necklaces out of clover, or how to play "Red Rover" and double hopscotch.

You won't understand why they never overcame the temptation of putting their fingers in the cake icing when you weren't looking or of bringing you freshly picked flowers from your neighbor's prized flower garden. You won't again fully share their excitement or participate with them when they try to see how high they can swing, how dizzy they can get on the merry-go-round after they have eaten, or how fast they can go down steep snow-covered hills "bellybuster" on their sleds.

There will come a day when you will see grass growing under their swing set and in their sandbox. You will not have any reason for buying Easter egg dye, birthday candles, Halloween costumes, Christmas dolls, or toy trucks. You will not understand why you cling to your child a little longer than you should on that first day of school or why you cry when your son receives his high school diploma or when your daughter tries on her wedding dress.

None of this sounds real to you because you're in the stage of new beginnings, you're only considering "now." In time your house will be quiet. You will have two place settings at the kitchen table. The baby bed, stroller, highchair, playpen, and wading pool will be stowed in the attic with boxes of report cards, homemade Mother's Days cards, school papers, awards, roller skates, football equipment, and dolls.

You have and will play many roles in your lifetime. As you have time to review them, you're going to realize that the lasting values you have learned had their beginnings when you held your babies in your arms, thinking of their interests rather than your own, learning from them, seeing them find their place in the world. When your house settles into unaccustomed silences, somehow your children's influence will continue to penetrate its walls, and you will feel satisfied and blessed.

In the strange silence of a late afternoon in years that are to come, you may, for the first time since you became a mother, have time to begin to comprehend what it has meant to give yourself wholly, totally committing your life to caring for another human being.

Postnatal Exercises

1. Laugh at least once a day.
2. Make the necessary arrangements in order for you to resign from parenting fifteen minutes each day.
3. Express to your husband and baby no less than once a day, "I love you."
4. Before you get out of bed each morning, ask God to mold you into the kind of mom He wants you to be for that day.
5. Tell God how much you love Him for allowing you to be a mother.